THE STEP-BY-STEP TRAINING MANUAL OF

SOCCER SKILLS & TECHNIQUES

This edition is published by Armadillo, an imprint of Anness Publishing Ltd,
108 Great Russell Street, London WC1B 3NA; info@anness.com

www.annesspublishing.com; twitter: @Anness_Books

PUBLISHER'S NOTE

Although the advice and information in this book are believed to be accurate and true at the time of going to press, neither the authors nor the publisher can accept any legal responsibility or liability for any errors or omissions that may have been made nor for any inaccuracies nor for any loss, harm or injury that comes about from following instructions or advice in this book.

Manufacturer: Anness Publishing Ltd, Blaby Road, Wigston, Leicestershire LE18 4SE, England
For Product Tracking go to: www.annesspublishing.com/tracking
Batch: 5390-23830-1127

THE STEP-BY-STEP TRAINING MANUAL OF
SOCCER SKILLS & TECHNIQUES

INTRODUCTION

Soccer is one of the most popular sports in the world today. Its players are men and women, boys and girls, from six continents but they all have one thing in common. From the superstar professionals to the children playing in the street, every soccer player must practise in order to improve the skills which make the game so exciting.

Soccer Skills and Techniques aims to provide a comprehensive training manual for players and coaches alike.

Expert-approved training drills are demonstrated by professional coaches at The Bobby Charlton Soccer School in Manchester, England, to enable any player to develop essential skills. The step-by-step guides make every technique, from the basics to professional level, easy to learn and to perfect.

CONTENTS

Part 1

WORLD-CLASS SKILLS

Build your confidence on the ball with skills for all areas of the pitch, from the basics to match-winning tricks.

Passing basics

Coaches often say, 'If you can't pass, you can't play,' and it's true. Passing is the most important of all basic soccer skills. Precise passing enables your team to keep possession and build up goal attempts.

The passer's aim is to get the ball to the receiver quickly and accurately. The simplest way to do this is with the push pass, hit purposefully with the inside of the foot.

The ultimate goal

Good passes are weighted to land just in front of the receiver so he can take the ball without breaking stride. If possible, keep the ball moving forward - possession play is all very well, but your team's aim is to move upfield and score.

Coach says

- **Pass the ball but don't pass the responsibility. Pass to get yourself out of trouble by all means – but not if it puts the receiver in the same situation.**
- **Communicate constantly. Team-mates should shout or signal so that the player on the ball is aware of his best passing option.**

Basics Push the pass

For passes of up to 25m or so, the push pass is the most accurate. Plant your standing foot beside the ball and strike it in the middle with the inside of your foot, so that it rolls to the receiver. Make sure you follow through in the same direction as the pass.

Note that with this technique, you will not get as much leverage to drive the ball powerfully over long distances. Most players use the top of the foot to play longer balls.

1 Watching the ball, the player plants his standing foot alongside it.

2 He strikes the middle of the ball with the inside of his foot and it rolls to the receiver.

3 The passer follows through with his kicking foot towards the target of his pass.

Practice drill

Practise the accuracy of your passing with a team-mate in this easy drill. Stand 10m apart and pass the ball back and forth using the push pass.

To hone your skills further, bring in a third player to stand with his legs apart, midway between you and your team-mate. Now keep passing the ball to and fro with precision through his legs.

Keep the drill flowing. If you miss, just keep passing, and if you hit the middle player's legs, have him kick the ball back to one of the passers. Rotate positions every so often.

Skills check

- ○ Anticipation
- ○ Balance
- ○ Timing
- ○ Accuracy

Pass the ball carefully to and fro. Watch your foot as it moves on to the ball.

Follow through your pass to push it precisely through the player's legs.

Advanced Pass in a triangle

Three players each stand at one corner of a 10 x 10m square and pass the ball between them while a 'piggy in the middle' defender puts pressure on the players and intercepts their passes.

Try to keep the drill moving at speed – play one-touch passes if possible, but don't lose control of the ball.

1 As the defender in blue closes him down, the attacker lays the ball off to his team-mate.

2 The receiver prepares to make his pass, as the defender turns to close him down.

3 With the defender closing in, quick thinking is needed to make the next pass.

Ball control with the feet

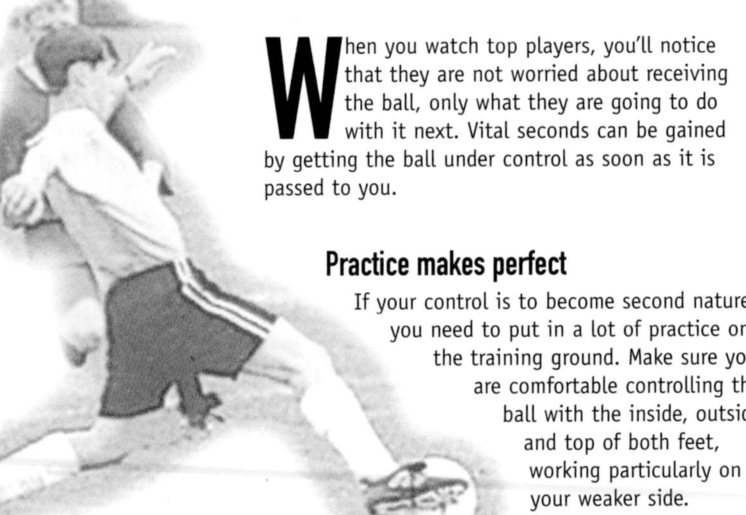

When you watch top players, you'll notice that they are not worried about receiving the ball, only what they are going to do with it next. Vital seconds can be gained by getting the ball under control as soon as it is passed to you.

Practice makes perfect

If your control is to become second nature, you need to put in a lot of practice on the training ground. Make sure you are comfortable controlling the ball with the inside, outside and top of both feet, working particularly on your weaker side.

Coach says

- Decide early what part of the foot you are going to use to control the ball.
- Don't get the ball caught underneath your feet. Make sure your first touch nudges the ball slightly ahead of you, so you can pass, shoot or move away.

Basics Cushion the ball

Practise controlling the ball by having a friend pass to you or by hitting the ball against a wall. Use different parts of your foot to stop the ball and nudge it in front of you, ready to play on. To take the pace off the ball and bring it fully under control, let the ball come to you – don't push at it.

INSIDE OF THE FOOT
As this player shows, the easiest way to control the ball is with the inside of the foot. It provides a long barrier to block the ball.

OUTSIDE OF THE FOOT
To make a quick turn, use the outside of your foot. Having controlled the ball, the player here can now turn to his right.

TOP OF THE FOOT
To use the top of your foot, point your toes downwards. Use this technique to push the ball forward and move off quickly.

Skills check

- Good feel for the ball
- Quick footwork
- Ability to use both feet
- Good balance
- Composure

Practice drill

In this drill, three players stand at three corners of a 10 x 10m square and pass a ball to each other in turn. After passing, each player runs to the empty corner. The players must control the ball quickly to set themselves up to play a comfortable pass. Run the drill for five minutes at a time.

1 Having received a pass from player C, player A controls the ball before...

2 ... passing to player B. As B controls the pass, A runs to the empty corner.

Advanced Control it under pressure

1 The green player receives a difficult ball, but he is able to bring it under control with the inside of his foot.

2 Having cushioned the ball, he pushes it on, bursts through the blue defence and heads for goal.

Now transfer your skills to a practice match. Two teams of three play each other on a 20 x 20m grid. Each team has two 1m-wide goals to attack, each one at a corner of the grid.

The two sides must pass or dribble their way up the grid to score. As the game is played in a small area, players will have little time on the ball before they are challenged. It is essential, therefore, that every player brings the ball under control instantly, so that they give themselves an extra split-second to decide on their next move. Don't forget to try and use both feet.

Running with the ball

The ability to run with the ball marks out the really good player from the average one. Strength and speed are needed if you want to take the ball forward, beat defenders and force your way into the danger zone. It is also very important to have good awareness – there is no point running into trouble!

Unlocking the defence

Players that can run with the ball can change the course of a game, upping the tempo and unlocking the most organised of defences. Defenders can benefit from developing this skill too. The sight of an accomplished centre back breaking out of defence and heading for goal can strike fear into opponents.

Coach says

- Aim to keep the ball a metre or so in front of you.
- Keep your arms out wide to maintain your balance.
- Don't let a player chasing you affect your concentration.
- Use both sides of each foot to control the ball and help you change direction.

Basics Keep control of the ball

You can practise this skill by yourself in a park. It is simply a case of running 30m or so with the ball at your feet. At first, you should concentrate on keeping the ball under control. Then work on increasing your speed, whilst still maintaining good control.

If you can get some friends to be defenders, it will be an even more rewarding exercise. The defenders can put pressure on the player running with the ball.

1 Use the outside of your foot or your instep (laces) to push the ball 2-3m. Accelerate quickly after it.

2 Keep your head up so your can run players around you. check the position of the ball by glancing down.

3 Use long strides, pump your arms and pick up your knees to increase your speed – without losing the ball.

Practice drill

To do this drill, you need at least one team-mate. The more people involved, the more effective the exercise will be. Mark three 10 x 10m grids about 25m apart from each other. Give each grid a name or number, then follow these steps:

1 Taking a ball each, all players dribble within one of the grids.

2 One player starts by calling out a grid name.

3 It's then a race to see who gets to that grid first. The winner calls the next name.

Advanced Perform under pressure

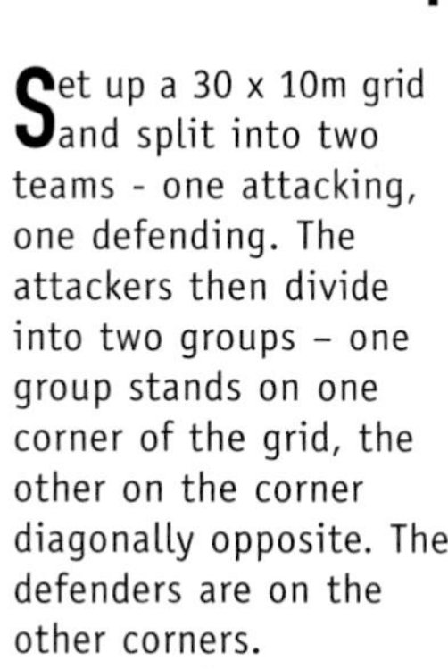

Set up a 30 x 10m grid and split into two teams - one attacking, one defending. The attackers then divide into two groups – one group stands on one corner of the grid, the other on the corner diagonally opposite. The defenders are on the other corners.

An attacker runs the ball along the 30m line, chased by a defender from the corner to his left. He passes to the next attacker, who sets off along his line. Continue until all the attackers have had a go.

Skills check

- ○ Balance and pace
- ○ Spatial awareness
- ○ Good co-ordination

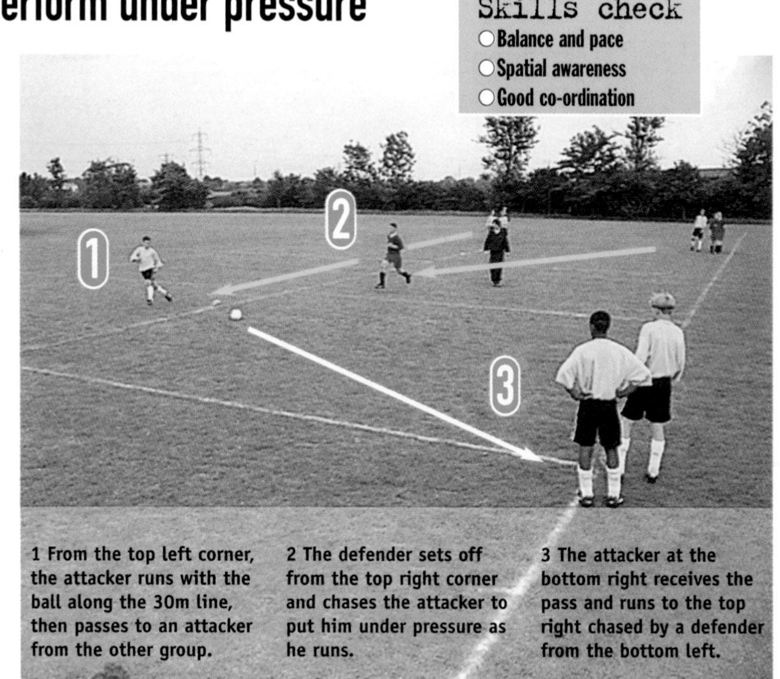

1 From the top left corner, the attacker runs with the ball along the 30m line, then passes to an attacker from the other group.

2 The defender sets off from the top right corner and chases the attacker to put him under pressure as he runs.

3 The attacker at the bottom right receives the pass and runs to the top right chased by a defender from the bottom left.

Screening the ball

When under pressure, it is vital that you can screen the ball by using your body to hold off an opponent when the ball is at or near your feet.

You will often see defenders screening the ball to stop a striker getting it before it goes out for a goal-kick. Attackers screen the ball even more frequently – often to buy time to weigh up their options. They might hold up the ball while holding off their marker before laying it off to a team-mate or turning to go for goal.

Keep the ball close

Be careful to screen the ball only if it is within playing distance. If not, the referee may penalise you for obstruction.

Coach says

- When the ball comes at you, always be on your toes so you can control it easily.
- With the ball at your feet, steady yourself and get low so the defender can't push you off the ball.
- Be aware of your options, even if under pressure.

Basics Hold him off

This is a simple drill designed to get you used to both receiving a pass under pressure and using your body to screen the ball from a close defender. Use your arms to make your body wider and stick out your backside.

The player screening the ball receives a pass to his feet. He is marked from behind and must control the ball, hold off the defender's challenge and return the ball crisply and accurately to the feeder.

1 The attacker stays ahead of his marker to make sure he is first to the ball.

2 Using his arms, he makes his body into as big a barrier as possible to fend off the defender.

3 Despite being tightly marked, his screening skill has enabled him to play the ball back easily.

Practice drill

On a 40 x 30m grid, two teams of three (plus goalkeepers) play against each other. A goal cannot be scored unless someone has screened the ball first.

This means the main striker is forced to play with his back to goal and must make himself available. When he receives the ball, he can turn his man or lay it off for someone else to shoot.

Skills check

- Good control
- Balance
- Strength on the ball
- Resilience

Control the ball and hold the marker off while weighing up the options.

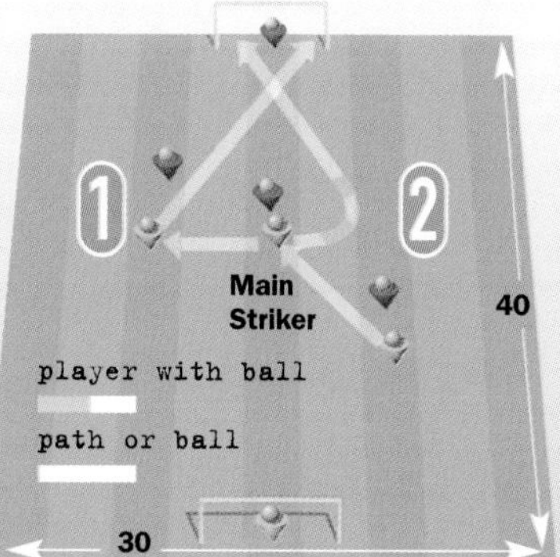

Once the main striker has screened the ball, he can either lay the ball off to a supporting team-mate (1) or turn his marker and get a shot in (2).

Advanced Look for support

In this drill, played on half a pitch, four attackers and a feeder play three defenders and a goalkeeper.

The feeder starts the drill by playing the ball to an attacker who has his back to goal and is closely marked by one of the defenders. The attacker must first screen the ball, keeping his marker at bay. He then can either turn and shoot, or lay the ball off into the path of one of the other two attackers – or the feeder – for them to strike at goal.

1 The ball is fed into the feet of the striker, who has come off his man.

2 He has his arms out and a good body shape to screen the ball.

3 Assessing his options, he rolls the ball into the path of a team-mate.

4 The supporting player races on to the pass and has a shot at goal.

Intercepting

This is the most effective way of getting the ball from the opposition. If a defender predicts a pass and acts quickly, he can win the ball cleanly and start a counter-attack. Intervening like this leaves opposition players wrong-footed and buys you time and space. Tackling – by comparison – is risky: you can give away a foul and you might end up out of position or stranded on the ground.

Coach says

- Opportunities to intercept happen all over the pitch. Defenders, midfielders and strikers should all practise intercepting skills.

Turn defence into attack

Although it is often considered a defensive skill, intercepting can win a match. If a quick-thinking striker intercepts a pass in the attacking third of the pitch, he can usually force a quick goal attempt before the defence has time to recover.

Skills check

- Awareness and anticipation
- Explosive pace
- Body strength

Basics Pounce on the pass

If you're marking a player, you'll often be just behind him. When he is passed to, you must be ready to dash out to intercept the ball.

This drill uses a metal man – you could use a sports bag instead, but you must run around it, not step over it. An attacker passes to the metal man; a defender waits behind it. When the pass is played, the defender must get to the ball before it reaches the metal man, and try to get it under control with one touch.

The defender anticipates the attacker's pass and bursts out from behind the metal man to intercept it.

Practice drill

Now replace the metal man with a real opponent and try to intercept the pass. The defender must anticipate the ball being played and get out from behind his opponent to win it.

This drill helps you to decide when to intercept and when to cover. If you can't get to the ball first, remain behind the attacker and tackle him later.

1 As the pass is played, the defender and an attacker both move towards the ball. The defender is on his toes...

2 ...which enables him to get away fastest. Once in front, he uses his body strength to stay ahead of the attacker.

3 He gets to the ball first, controls it, then passes it back. The drill is repeated 10 times, then players swap positions.

Advanced Intercept and counter-attack

To learn to turn defence into attack, two teams of seven play on a small-size pitch (below). Only one attacker and one defender can go into each of the 15m 'end zones'. The defenders must try to intercept passes to the attackers, then either run the ball forward or pass. If he chooses to run forward, a team-mate takes his place in the end zone.

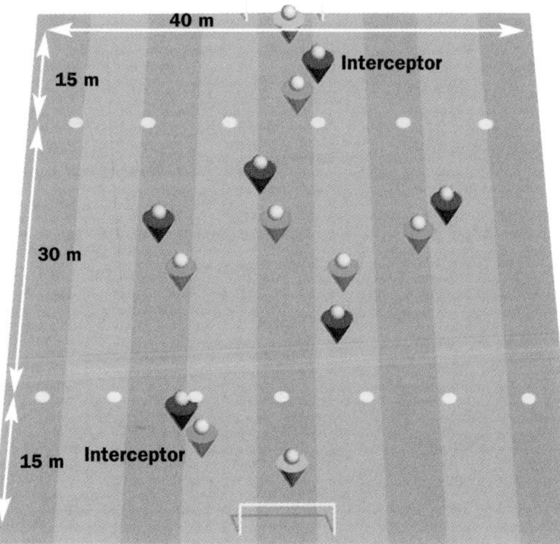

The pale blue defender intercepts a pass to the dark blue attacker in the 15m end zone. He can then pass or run forward to counter-attack. If the attacker wins the ball and scores, he swaps places with a team-mate.

Tackling basics

Dispossessing your opponent is the primary aim of tackling. If possible, you should emerge from the tackle with the ball, but as long as you prevent your opponent making progress, your job is done.

Adjust your technique

When an opponent is running straight at you, it is best to use the inside of your foot to block the ball. Keep your blocking ankle rigid, lean in and make a clean strike.

With side tackles, pivot on the foot nearest to your opponent, while you swing your other foot around to block the ball.

Do not tackle from behind. You are liable to be penalised even if you make contact with the ball.

Coach says

- **Be patient. Only tackle if you're sure you can win the ball. You don't want to be left stranded while your opponent gets through. And once you spot your chance, take it.**
- **Block and harry the attacker. You might force him into a mistake, giving you a chance to make a tackle and take the ball.**

Basics Win the ball

An attacker and a defender stand at opposite sides of a 10 x 10m square. The attacker's aim is to run the ball to the other side of the square. The defender's aim is to dispossess him.

The defender should run in and jockey the attacker at arm's length. When he sees his chance, he should make a quick, clean tackle.

Don't stand too close to the attacker. Bend your knees slightly and try to stay on your feet.

1 The defender approaches the attacker. As he arrives, he slows down, keeping a metre or two away.

2 The defender adopts the ready stance: knees bent, facing his opponent at an angle and watching the ball.

3 When the attacker takes the ball forward, the defender quickly extends his foot to poke it away.

Practice drill

Skills check
- Stable posture
- Timing
- Strength
- Concentration

This drill takes part in a 20 x 30m zone and needs a goalkeeper, a defender and at least two attackers. The attackers queue up at the 30m line. They run the ball up one by one and try to get past the defender and score.

The defender is awarded a point for delaying an attacker and two points if he wins the ball. Win or lose, each attacker runs round to the back after each go and lines up for his next turn.

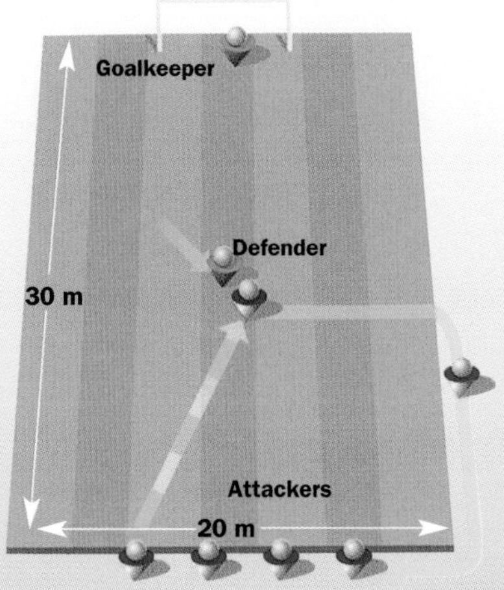

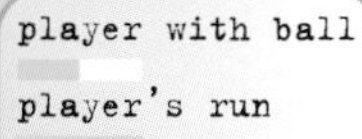

The defender (in pale blue) tackles the attacker and wins the ball. The attacker must then run to the back of the queue.

Advanced Make the tackle count

Six attackers with a ball each are tackled by two defenders in a 20 x 20m area. The defenders have to dispossess each attacker in the shortest possible time. As each attacker loses the ball, he drops out.

The defenders can work together – with one tackling while the other provides cover. If the attacker beats the first man, he runs into the second defender.

1 The attacker (in dark blue) has fooled the first defender and takes the ball past him.

2 The second defender is in position behind his team-mate and ready to challenge for the ball.

3 Seeing an opening, he pounces on the ball. The attacker is out of the game.

Beating an outfield player

Every successful attacking team has players with the ability to take on and beat their markers one-on-one. Some use mouth-watering skills to outfox their opponents, others destroy them with sheer pace.

However it is achieved, beating an outfield player takes an opposition player out of the game and creates the time and space needed to move the attack forward.

Ready for the next stage

The methods used to beat outfield players are perfected on the training ground, but the world's most gifted players are able to transfer what they've practised to the high pressure situations they experience in matches.

Coach says

- Running at an outfield player puts him under pressure – look to take advantage if he is caught off balance or expecting you to pass.

Skills check

- Vision and awareness
- Use of turns and tricks
- Excellent close control
- Explosive acceleration

Basics Go past your man

This drill encourages you to experiment as you take on your opponent in a one-on-one situation. Three attackers and three defenders face each other from opposite corners of a 20 x 20m grid.

In turn, each attacker brings out the ball, takes on the defender who moves forward to block him and tries to reach the opposite corner. Use your acceleration and turning skills.

1 The attacker (in pale blue) sets off for the opposite corner, always aware of the space he has available to try to beat his marker.

2 Keeping the ball under control, he then makes his move – hooking the ball with the inside of his foot to unbalance his opponent.

3 He accelerates clear, and brings the ball quickly under control again. Next time, he should try a different move to beat the player.

Practice drill

Beating an opponent in a one-on-one situation calls for skill, pace and invention. In this drill, players attempt firstly to beat a single opponent, then move on to a two-versus-two scenario.

They can use a variety of methods: maybe putting the ball through the defender's legs to 'nutmeg' him or simply knocking the ball past him to beat him with sheer pace.

Three attackers and three defenders – each numbered one to three – line up on opposite sides of a 20 x 20m grid. The coach calls out a number and the two players who share it come on to the grid. The attacker then has to cross the grid and beat his defender while staying in the square.

Advanced Rush to goal

In this drill for two players, the attacker must beat a defender, then shoot on goal. The defender stands on the edge of the penalty box; the attacker stands 5m back from him. He then tries to beat the defender and score. To practise from all angles, the players should repeat the drill at the left edge, right edge and centre of the penalty box, then swap positions.

1 The attacker hooks the ball to the left with the outside of his foot, unbalancing the defender.

2 He then tries to accelerate away from the defender into space before he can react.

3 The attacker makes just enough room for himself to get in a powerful shot at goal.

Hitting the target

It sounds obvious, but the most important skill when you are shooting is to make sure you hit the target. It doesn't matter how hard you strike the ball, if it ends up going wide of the post or over the bar, you should see it as an opportunity wasted.

Challenge the keeper

If it is true that hard shots are difficult to save, it is also true that they are difficult to control. So it is important to work on accuracy first, then power. Constant practice will hone your instinct for choosing the best angle. If a shot is on target, you have always got a chance of scoring – the keeper can make a mistake on the weakest of shots.

Coach says

- Keep your composure when a shooting chance comes your way. Don't panic and 'snatch' at the ball – strike it confidently.
- Point your toes downwards as you strike a bouncing ball – this will help keep the shot low.
- At close range, accuracy is often more important than power, so try shooting with the side of the foot rather than with the laces.

Basics Kick the ball correctly

Get your shots on target by concentrating on technique.

1 Plant your non-striking foot at the side of the ball, your knee slightly bent, and arms out for balance. Lean over the ball slightly.

2 Keeping your eyes on the ball, strike it through the centre with the part of the foot that is covered by the laces – the instep.

3 Make sure you follow through in a straight line with your kicking leg, to keep the shot accurate and add more power.

Skills check

- Ability to use both feet
- Good balance
- Awareness of the goal's position, even if behind you

Practice drill

Get together with a partner and set up a goal, using cones as markers. Stand opposite each other about 15-20m either side of the goal-line.

One of you shoots at the goal, the other retrieves the ball and shoots it back.

As your accuracy improves, you can make the goal narrower. Try shots with both feet and from a variety of angles.

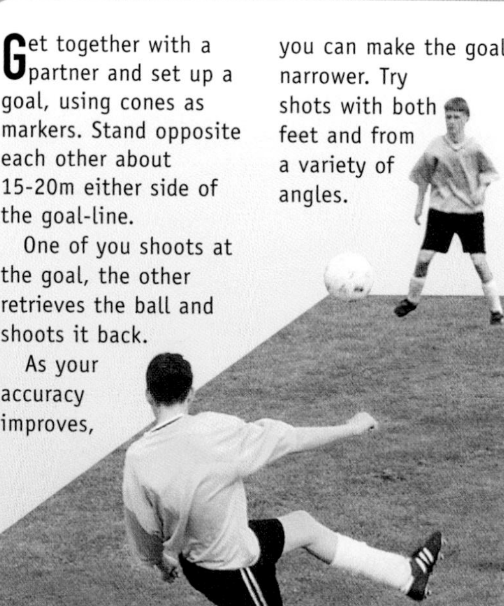

Timed practice

Start from the marker. Run up and hit the right-hand ball low into the goal with your right foot.

Race back around the marker, then run up and strike the left-hand ball with your left foot.

As you go back around the marker, your partner races into goal to try to save your third shot. Hit the central ball with either foot but aim to shoot it low and into the corner.

Time the drill, then change over and see who is quickest. For every shot missed or saved, add five seconds on to your time.

Advanced Make it hard for the keeper

When shooting, you should aim for one corner of the goal and try to keep the ball low. It is easier for a goal-keeper to stretch for a high shot than to get down to a low one. In fact, a low shot close to a keeper can often cause him more problems than a high shot which is further away from him.

Tracking back

Chasing back quickly from attack to defence is one of the most important skills in the modern game. As teams get players forward to support attacks, the opposition often attempts to soak up pressure then break forward quickly to score. Tracking back well denies them the opportunity to mount effective counter-attacks.

Never say die

The skill demands the ability to change direction quickly then run at top speed – possibly for the length of the pitch. Determination is vital, too, as is the ability to tackle well. Every player must learn how to do it; even defenders will be required to track back when they go up for set pieces.

Coach says

- **Never give up when tracking back. Even if you don't make a tackle, the pressure may make the attacker hurry his pass, cross or shot.**

Skills check

- Turning ability
- Speed
- Stamina
- Determination
- Tackling ability

Basics Chase and tackle

To track back well, players have to turn and chase at speed. This drill involves two sets of players and uses a 10 x 30m grid with a 1m-wide goal at one end. One player (A) from the first set dribbles past two metal men (or cones) and passes to player (B) in the second set. Player A now has to track back and tackle B before he scores a goal. The drill repeats with player C dribbling upfield.

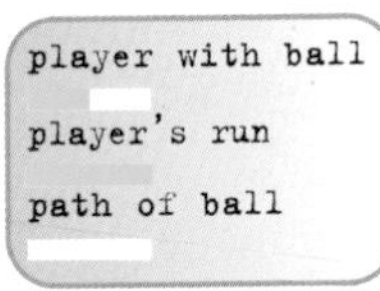

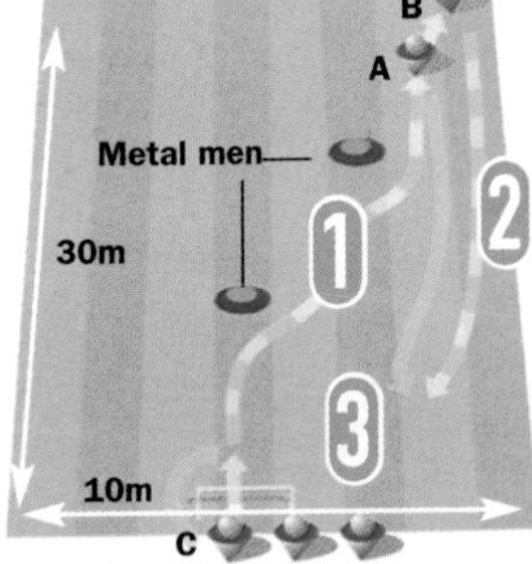

1 Dribble past the metal men. As you pass the last one, lay the ball off to the waiting player.

2 As he takes it and sprints back up the pitch, turn and accelerate to track back with him.

3 Get level with your opponent and then attempt to tackle him. Don't tackle from behind.

Practice drill

In this drill players practise tracking back on a full-size pitch with a keeper in goal. An attacker (in dark blue below) starts 40m from goal, faced by a tracking player. He knocks the ball through his opponent's legs. The tracking player must turn and chase the player with the ball to try to stop him scoring.

The attacker is free to shoot from any distance, so it is up to the tracking player to get close to the striker as quickly as he can. He must try to tackle and regain possession if possible. The two players should take it in turns to be the attacker and the defender.

1 The attacker (in dark blue) hits the ball through the legs of his opponent.

2 As the attacker bursts forward after the ball, the tracking player turns.

3 The player tracking back uses acceleration to catch the attacker.

4 With speed and determination, he gets in a position to make a tackle.

Advanced Force play your way

Tracking back does not always lead to a tackling opportunity.

In this seven-a-side match played on half a pitch, the aim is to force the opposition to play the ball out wide.

When one team gains possession, the other team should track back and get behind the ball, shutting off all options bar the pass or a run into wide areas.

One player must get close to apply pressure, while his team-mates must cover and close down options. If play is forced out to the wings, defenders are in a superb position to win back possession.

The blue attacker has been forced wide but is moving at speed. Now the pressurising defender must track back quickly to close him down. Another defender adds cover.

Jockeying the attacker

Few things make life easier for an attacker than a defender who dives in. A good forward will see an impatient challenge coming, dodge round it and leave the defender stranded.

Stall the attack

A defender's first task is to delay the attacker by 'jockeying' him – keeping his body between the attacker and the goal, backing off slightly as the attacker comes forward and waiting for the right moment to tackle.

This causes the attack to lose its momentum and gives the other players time to get back and defend.

Coach says

- Any defender who charges into tackles without thinking is a liability to his team. He gives his side no chance to regroup.
- Don't make it easy for the attacker. Bide your time and concentrate on the ball, not the movements of the attacker.

Basics Stay on your toes

Good jockeying relies on five key points. (1) Keep your opponent in front of you. (2) Keep your body between the attacker and the goal. (3) Always turn sideways so it is harder for the striker to put the ball through your legs. (4) Stay on your toes to make sharp changes of direction. (5) Keep your opponent at arm's length – so you're at a good distance to get a tackle in.

The coach exhibits the five basic skills used in keeping a forward at bay

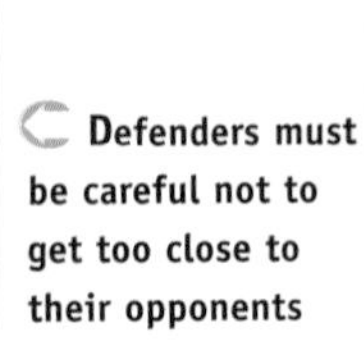

Defenders must be careful not to get too close to their opponents

Practice drill

This is a one-on-one drill played in a 10 x 20m grid. The attacker attempts to beat the defender and score past a goalkeeper defending a 5m-wide goal. The defender's job is to hold the attacker up, force him away from goal and get in a tackle if he can. Here, the defender manoeuvres the attacker wide of goal, allowing him no space to come inside.

The defender moves closer

Side-on, he keeps his eye on the ball ...

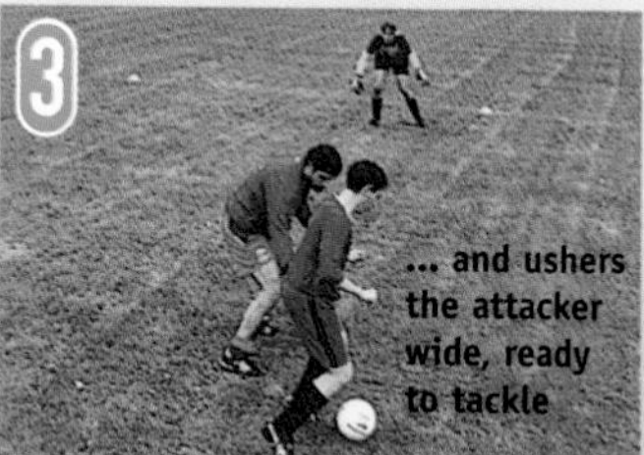

... and ushers the attacker wide, ready to tackle

Advanced Make communication the key

Once you have worked on the core skill, you must combine it with communication.

This drill is two versus two on a 10 x 20m grid. Starting at opposite ends, the attackers (in blue) have to find a way past the defenders (in green) who try to win the ball. One defender jockeys the attacker on the ball, while the other picks up the spare man. They should switch roles after 10 minutes.

Defender A prepares to jockey the attacker with the ball ...

... while defender B follows the second attacker's run

Skills check

- Positional sense
- Quick reactions
- Composure
- Quick feet

Defensive headers

Any defender dealing with a high ball must first make sure it doesn't bounce. If the ball bounces, it stays in the danger area longer and gives the attacker more chance to take advantage. Heading the ball clear first time is the quickest and most effective way for a defender to defuse this dangerous situation.

Attack the ball

Whatever your height, you need determination, athleticism, timing and good positioning. Read the game, so you can get in a good position. Be first to the ball and attack it as early in its flight as you can. Head the ball hard, high, long and wide. That way, even if the opposition picks up your clearance, you give your team time to recover and to regroup.

Coach says

- Assess the path of the ball and try to meet it as early as possible.
- Learn how to jump higher for the ball by pushing off from one foot.

Skills check

- Aggression
- Determination
- Courage
- Timing
- Vigilance

Basics Head it high

When heading the ball in defence, your priorities are to get to the ball first and clear the ball as far away as possible from the danger zone.

Practise at first by throwing the ball up for yourself to head. Try to generate power by using all your body rather than just your head and neck.

Try to get good height on the header. Head through the bottom of the ball and make solid contact with your forehead.

1 The defender keeps his eye on the ball and bends his knees, ready for take off.

2 As the ball drops, he throws his arms forwards to propel himself into the air.

3 He then throws his arms backwards to push his head firmly 'through' the ball.

Practice drill

This simple drill requires only three players – two standing 10m apart with one in the middle acting as an obstacle. The distance between the players can be extended as they get more proficient. The object is for each player to clear the centre man with his header and direct the ball to his opposite number. If a player is unable to head the full distance, he goes in the middle.

1 Throw the ball up just in front of yourself and keep your eye on it. Time your jump so you meet the ball at the highest point possible.

2 To get your header over the centre player, strike through the bottom of the ball with your forehead. Tense your neck muscles as you head the ball.

Advanced Beat the striker

Now practise defensive heading with the pressure of an attacker. In this drill, three attackers play against two defenders and a goalkeeper.

The first attacker acts as a feeder, playing the ball out to the second attacker on the wing. The winger then crosses the ball high into the penalty area, where the third attacker is ready to head it.

One of the two defenders patrolling the penalty area must deal with the cross when it comes in. He must anticipate the flight of the ball, get to it before the attacker, and head it as high and as far as possible.

When the ball comes into the penalty area the defender (in green) must clear the danger

1 Attack the ball with confdence and aggression. Be first to the ball and take the initiative.

2 Meet the ball early and make strong contact to power your clearance well away from the box.

The slide tackle

A slide tackle is one of the most difficult defensive skills to learn. But – when done properly – it is hard to beat for sheer effectiveness. Once developed, this skill will add an extra dimension to your game – and help strengthen the defensive qualities of your team.

Consider the risks

It is wise to use the slide tackle as a last resort because it involves going to ground and takes you out of the game for a short time. And unfortunately, it is easy to foul an opponent and give away a free kick in a dangerous area. If you can't make contact with the ball, don't even attempt a slide tackle. After making the tackle, try to react quickly and get to your feet as soon as you can.

Coach says

- Keep your eye on the ball rather than on your opponent
- Approach from the side – not from behind.
- Push the ball as far away from your opponent as possible.
- Get straight back on to your feet again.

Basics Go to ground and make the tackle

Practise this drill, in which the attacker and defender start side by side. The attacker kicks the ball 5m in front of him. The defender must reach the ball first, slide in for the tackle from the side and either kick the ball away from the attacker or come up with it himself.

1 As you approach the ball from the side, begin to lower your body. Always keep your eyes on the ball.

2 Slide in on your inside leg, using your inside arm as support. Swing your tackling leg to the front of the ball.

3 Once the tackle is complete, use your inside arm to lever yourself up and get back onto your feet quickly, with the ball if you can.

Practice drill

1 Do not attempt the tackle from behind the attacker – this will result in a foul.

2 When you are ahead of the attacker, you are far more likely to take the ball cleanly.

When performing this tackle, it is vital to make contact with the ball – NOT the man. You must be at least level with the attacker before you slide, as any tackle from behind is judged a foul.

It is well worth practising this skill over and over, just to make sure you can time it well before using it in a match.

In this drill, the defender in green starts a metre behind the attacker in blue. The defender's job is to catch the attacker before making the tackle. Try running over shorter distances to increase your pace. To be successful, you must be committed to chase the man down and win the ball.

Advanced Retain possession

Although a slide tackle will usually just kick the ball away from your attacker, practise keeping the ball after your tackle.

Try to wrap your instep around the ball (right) as you make contact, in order to keep possession for your team.

Skills check

- Bravery
- Timing
- Co-ordination
- Speed
- Agility

1 As you reach your opponent, slide onto your non-tackling leg. Wrap your other foot around the ball.

2 Having got the ball under control, get to your feet as quickly as possible and bring it out of the danger zone.

Dribbling

Few sights excite a crowd as much as fine dribbling skills. Done well, dribbling is magical to watch – and is a potent attacking weapon. The key is good ball control, as well as speed and being comfortable moving off either foot.

Control and acceleration

Good dribblers have complete control of the ball and are able to move in any direction – and at speed. Equally important is their ability to step up a gear to accelerate away from their opponents. A player on a dribbling run can cause great concern to the opposition. He will often be shadowed by more than one defender. This means that a good dribbler has at least one team-mate free for a pass.

Coach says

- Choose the correct time and place on the pitch to go on a dribbling run.
- Develop confidence to go in close to players so that once you have dribbled past them, they have no way back.

Basics Learn to use both feet

Good dribbling ability comes from practising ball control at speed. Once you master this, you will gain the confidence to take on and beat opponents.

Make sure you practise with both feet. If you can only dribble on one side, it becomes easier for defenders to close you down as they can predict which direction you will go in.

Concentrate on developing your balance, turning suddenly, making feints and accelerating off both feet. You will probably develop your own style – maybe short, quick steps, or long, elegant strides – there is no right or wrong way.

1 Two players stand either side of a line, between two cones that are placed 10m apart. Neither player is allowed to cross the line.

See if you can fool your opponent

2 Feinting and changing direction quickly, the green player has to dribble the ball to any cone before the blue player gets to the spot.

Practice drill

Six players in green, each with a ball, dribble within a 10 x 10m grid. On the coach's call, players use their right or left foot, speed up or slow down. Each player has to react quickly to the calls. More pressure is added with four defenders, who come in to tackle the dribblers. An attacker whose ball is kicked out is eliminated. The last dribbler in possession wins.

The dribblers have to avoid each other

Four defenders in blue attempt to tackle the dribblers

Advanced Take on the opposition

Transfer your dribbling skills into a match situation by using this advanced drill. A 30 x 20m pitch is marked out with three small goals at either end. Four green players face four players in blue.

Each team is allowed to score in any of the three opposition goals. This encourages players to change direction and use their dribbling skills to attack any goal, or to spot a team-mate better placed to dribble to it.

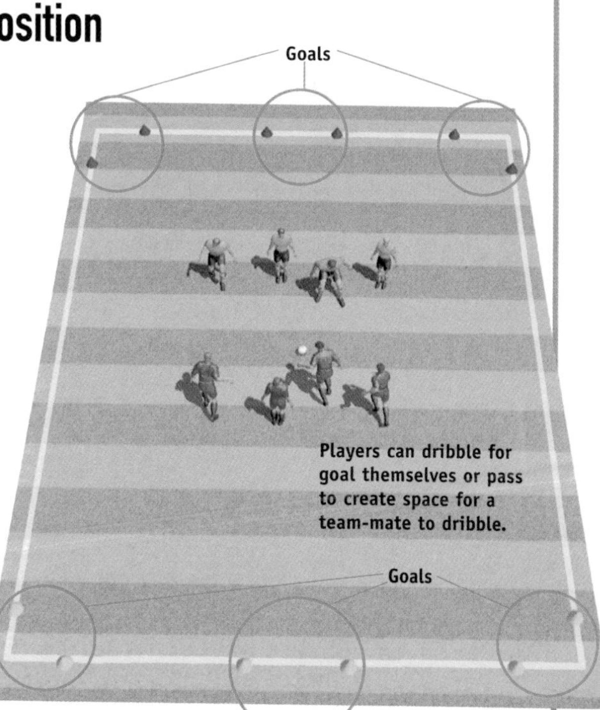

Coloured cones mark out three small goal options at each end.

Teams can score in any of the three opposition goals.

Skills check

- Control with both feet
- Good body swerves
- Effective disguising
- Ball trick skills
- Good pace
- Confidence
- Ability to change pace

Feinting

Also known as 'selling a dummy' or 'throwing a dummy', feinting is great way to trick a defender. You simply run the ball at your opponent, make as if to go one side of him, but actually go round him on the other side.

Exaggerated movement

To really 'sell' the feint, you need to exaggerate your body movement in the direction you are pretending to go. Plant your foot firmly and drop your shoulder to suggest you are going one way, then suddenly push off in the opposite direction.

Mastering the body action is quite easy. The difficult part is keeping control of the ball while you are doing it – so lots of practice is essential.

Coach says

- **Perfect the move on both sides of a defender, so you can keep him guessing each time.**
- **Don't try the feint when in defence – you could end up giving the ball to your opponents in a dangerous position.**

Basics Plant the foot and drop the shoulder

First practise the skill by using a cone marker as a 'defender' to build up your confidence in the move.

Make a real show of looking to go one way before exploding away in the opposite direction. Remember that the key is to maintain control of the ball at all times, as well as keep your balance.

Practise the feint both to the left and the right of the cone to develop your skills in both feet.

1 Run with the ball up to the marker. When 1–2m away from it, steady yourself to prepare for the feint.

2 Plant your left foot firmly and drop your left shoulder to look as if you are going to break to your left.

3 Push off sharply from your left foot and take the ball past the marker to the right. Accelerate away from the 'defender'.

Practice drill

1 The two players, each with a ball, approach a marker at pace. Both feint to go left, but actually move to the right.

2 The players accelerate away, keeping the balls under control. The drill repeats with a feint right and move left.

Try this drill with a team-mate. Run, with a ball each, towards one another. As you approach the central marker, you must feint past each other and then explode away into space. You must both decide beforehand whether to go left or right – or else you will risk running into each other!

Skills check

- Agility
- Good balance
- Dribbling skills
- Rapid acceleration

Advanced Get past the last man

Practise using your feinting skills in a match situation by setting up this pitch drill. You will need one feeder, two attackers, two defenders and a keeper. The feeder passes the ball to one of the attackers from the wing. The attacker has to beat his defender with a feinting movement, then go on to shoot.

The drill gives you confidence to try a feint and use the space.

1 An attacker in green receives and controls the feeder's pass, as his marker closes him down.

2 Dropping one shoulder to fool his marker, the attacker then rounds him and accelerates away.

3 The attacker is now one-on-one with the keeper and has created a chance to strike at goal.

The inside hook

Used to get yourself out of trouble or to get defences into it, the inside hook is a favoured move for players that love to take opponents on. It involves two basic elements – disguising the move by pretending to pass or shoot and drawing the defender in to make a block, then using the side of your foot to drag or 'hook' the ball across your body.

Cut and run

Faced with a defender between you and the goal, you can employ the inside hook to set up a shot. Farther out, you can use it to draw the defender and sprint away.

Coach says

- You need to make the defender believe you are going to hit the ball. Exaggerate your strike so he buys the dummy.
- Get your arms out to aid your balance and to sell the move.
- When you cut across the defender, get low down – this will make your turning sharper.

Basics Turn on the style

You can use the inside hook to get out of a difficult situation by adding a half turn to it. If you are running into a group of defenders, turn through 180° – shielding the ball with your body – then retreat in search of support. To practise this, run up to a marker or metal man, use the inside hook, turn 180° and then run back to the start. Keep the ball under control at all times.

1 As you run up to the metal man, fake to shoot but...

2 ...then stop, cut the ball across you and turn.

3 Get your body between the metal man and ball.

Practice drill

If you extend your turn through 360°, you can draw the defender around with you and explode away from him.

When the defender confronts you, he will be between you and the goal. After your hook and turn, he will be left behind as you sprint away.

Try the move slowly at first, then add snap to your turn when you are sure of the technique. Keep the ball tightly under control at all times, and stay low as you turn and begin your run.

1 Do the inside hook then turn full circle – 360°.

2 Drag the ball with you and run clear of the metal man.

Advanced Hook into a sharp turn

Practise the inside hook in a 10 x 20m grid. Attackers line up in one corner. One by one, they run up the line with the ball. From the diagonally opposite corner, a defender comes to challenge. The attacker draws him and then uses the inside hook to cut inside.

Skills check
- Quick feet
- Good control
- Pace
- Balance and body control

1 Draw the defender and make as if to shoot or pass.

2 As the defender begins his lunge, hook the ball.

3 Keep low and let the ball run on to your other foot.

4 Drive away from your low position into space.

The outside hook

The outside hook is a great way of getting rid of close-marking defenders. It demands agility, awareness and close ball control – but with practice it can easily be mastered.

To perform the move, you step over, or past, the ball and sweep it behind you with the outside of your foot. You then turn and take the ball in the opposite direction.

Screen the ball

The outside hook keeps your body between the ball and the defender, creating a shield. It is useful for wingers who need to get away from defenders to cross the ball or create a different angle of attack.

Coach says

- For balance, keep your body low, drop your shoulder and swivel your hips as you turn. Aim for a fast, flowing motion.
- Fooling your marker is vital. Think of planting one foot then hooking with the other as a type of feint or dummy.

Basics Hook yourself some space

First, practise the outside hook with a stationary ball to master the technique.

Plant your standing foot to the side, giving yourself room to swing your playing foot over, or past, the ball. Drop your shoulder (right if you are turning right, left if turning left) and hook the ball behind you with the outside of your playing foot, so that you can make a 180° turn on to it.

1 Having planted your standing foot alongside the ball...

2 ...swing your playing foot past it...

3 ...and turn away in the opposite direction. Now try it using your other foot.

Practice drill

1 Starting at the side of the square, run in fast with the ball under control.

2 As you get to the marker, do the outside hook and run the ball back to the next player.

Now practise with a moving ball. Place a marker in the middle of a 10 x 10m square. You need at least two players standing at each side of the square. One player from each side runs with the ball towards the marker, then turns round using the outside hook, turns and runs back to his partner.

The second player then takes the ball and repeats the move.

Advanced Turn out of trouble

In this open-play exercise, four attackers try to score against four defenders and a keeper on a 40 x 40m playing area. A point is scored for an outside hook as well as for a goal.

Try using the outside hook when you are running out of space – either when a defender is blocking your progress or when you are coming up to the byline.

1 As the attacker runs down the wing, a defender closes in and restricts the chances of making a cross.

2 Before the attacker reaches the byline, he uses the outside hook to turn back to evade the defender and find space.

3 The attacker's outside hook catches the defender flat-footed and buys some time to make a telling pass.

Skills check

- Good balance
- Fluid movement
- Speed on the turn
- Acceleration after the turn

The drag-back

Simple and relatively easy to master, the drag-back is one of the most effective attacking skills. Employed to outwit an opponent – especially in tight situations – the skill usually involves enticing a defender towards you, pulling the ball back with the sole of the foot and accelerating away.

Fast feet

To make the drag-back effective, you must perform it with pace and confidence. By encouraging the defender to commit, you can give yourself time and space to attack, while he tries to recover. Alternatively, you can make room for a shot on your favoured side. It is a technique that is great to watch and even more rewarding if you can perfect it and make it a part of your game.

Coach says

- Make your mind up in good time if you are going to use the drag back. Speed of thought is your best friend.
- Lure the defender in close so he is committed and off balance when you try the trick.
- Execute the drag-back swiftly and know what you are going to do after the move.

Basics Zip the ball back

To perform the drag-back well, you need to lure the defender in as close as possible, before dragging the ball out of his way. The key to this lies in swift and precise execution, with the ball under control so that you can move away quickly. Practise the move by yourself first.

Skills check

- Assured ball control
- Quick feet
- Turn of pace
- Excellent balance

1 Plant your non-kicking foot behind and to the side of the ball. This will enable you to retain your balance during the move.

2 Use the sole of your boot to grip the ball. Drag it back quickly, as if you were pulling it away from an onrushing opposing defender.

3 Pull back your foot to move the ball back about half a metre. You then have the time and space to push it away in another direction.

Practice drill

Use a cone to represent a defender in this solo drill and attack it at pace. As you close in on the cone, disguise the drag-back, perhaps by faking a shot or pass. Executing the move at speed, put your foot on top of the ball and drag it back. Then use the inside or outside of your foot to go left or right. Practise until you are comfortable going to either side.

1 Concentrate and keep the ball under control.

2 Use the sole of your foot to drag it back.

3 Pull your playing foot back and use it to...

4 ...push the ball off in the direction you want.

Advanced Take on the defender

Now practise with a team-mate. Take it in turns to be attacker and defender. The attacker should approach the defender fast but with the ball under control, use the drag-back and knock the ball to either side.

Having created some space, he can then try to accelerate away from the defender. Make sure you practise with both feet.

1 The attacker comes forward at pace, disguising his intentions.

2 He drags the ball behind his standing foot and then knocks it...

3 ...to his left. He has now created some space for himself.

The step-over

Step-overs look like fancy tricks, but they can be pure dynamite in the attacking third. The sudden blur of feet can leave defenders floundering or the keeper grasping at air. The step-over is basically an elaborate feint to put a defender off balance – you make as if to go one way, step over the ball and go the other way. Use it to create space for a cross, to fire a shot off, release a pass or go round the keeper.

Create the space

You can use the skill with the ball either stationary or moving in front of you. From a standing start, it opens up the chink of light needed to attack. Done at speed, it can take your marker out of the game.

Coach says

- **Get up on the balls of your feet so you can change direction easily.**
- **To wrong-foot the defender and gain the space you need, try to exaggerate the feint as you step over the ball.**

Basics Go feet first

Use a stationary ball to practise the skill slowly on your own until you have grasped the foot movements. Once you understand these, the step-over becomes easy to perform. When they become second nature, try doing them quickly.

Finally, try to do the step-over with a moving ball. Make sure it is travelling very slowly at first, then gradually increase the speed until the entire move becomes fluid and automatic.

1 **Stand with the ball in front of you. Make as if to kick it with the inside of your foot but lift your foot right over and across the ball instead.**

2 **The step-over foot should be kept low over the ball. Put it down on the other side of the ball and spring back from it.**

3 **Take the ball forwards and away in the opposite direction with the outside of the same foot. Stop the ball and try it again.**

The attacker shapes to go to his left, steps over the ball, and moves right

The defender follows the initial foot and body movement

Practice drill

The real test of this skill is if it gives you enough time to cross, pass or get a shot in on goal. This practice drill is all about using the step-over to score goals.

You need a goalkeeper and a defender – the rest of your group can be attackers. The defender waits on the penalty spot, while the attackers line up on the edge of the box. The attackers then take it in turns to run at the defender, try to beat him with a step-over, and use the space created to have a shot at goal.

When everyone has had a go, change the defender and goalkeeper and start again.

Advanced Practice against an opponent

Try the step-over against a team-mate. The attacker should approach the defender with the ball under control and use the step-over to go round him, then sprint away.

1 Push the ball slowly towards your opponent. Pressure from the defender should be minimal at first.

2 Shape as if to pass or shoot, but lift your foot over the ball instead and put it down on the far side.

3 Put your weight on to your step-over foot and push off strongly from it to change direction quickly.

4 Take the ball forwards and away with the outside of your step-over foot. Accelerate clear.

Skills check

- Quick feet
- Good balance
- Co-ordination
- Disguise your intentions
- Dropping of the shoulder
- Ability to suddenly change direction
- Control with the outside of the foot

The Cruyff turn

Named after the Dutch star of the 1970s, Johan Cruyff, the Cruyff turn is still deceiving defences today. The world first saw his trademark ploy at the 1974 World Cup, when his skills took Holland all the way to the final. With practice, you too can leave defenders trailing.

Fluid move

The turn enables you to change direction quickly and lose a close marker. In one movement, you flick the ball behind you with the inside of your foot and spin around to follow it.

Johan Cruyff often used the move on the wing to wrong-foot his markers, but it is equally effective in central attacking positions.

Coach says

- **Accelerating away at speed is vital. Even if you've made a perfect turn, a good defender will recover quickly. So make sure you're well away before he can react.**
- **Be aware of where the ball is at all times, so that you can turn to follow it and bring it under control. As with all ball skills, practice is the key.**

Basics Use a quick flick

First practise the Cruyff turn with a stationary ball. Concentrate on getting the foot movements right above all else.

Once you've got the hang of it, speed up and try dribbling a few paces before turning. When you have turned, really explode away. Work on disguise too – bring your kicking foot back sharply so it seems that you are going to hit the ball forward rather than flick it backwards.

1 Place your standing foot past the ball and draw back the opposite leg, as if you are about to pass or shoot.

2 Swing the kicking foot over the ball, and use the inside of the foot to flick the ball behind the other leg.

3 Turn in one smooth movement so you are facing in the opposite direction, ready to accelerate away.

Practice drill

Now try doing the Cruyff turn while running with the ball. Set out two markers, about 5m apart. Start at one marker and dribble the ball to the other one. Turn smoothly and dribble back, repeating the drill 10 times in each direction.

As you progress, try to increase your speed and keep the drill going so that your movements become more fluid.

1 Run at three-quarter speed with the ball at your feet.

2 On reaching the marker, flick the ball behind you and turn.

3 Dribble back to the first marker, ready to turn again.

Advanced Turn on the run

Once you've perfected the Cruyff turn itself, try performing the technique with the added pressure of a close-marking defender. With a team-mate, take turns to be attacker and defender. The attacker should try to catch the defender out with his Cruyff turn.

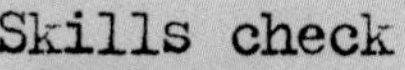

Skills check

- Good disguise
- Smooth movement
- Speed of execution
- Quick getaway

1 With the defender in close attendance, the attacker runs forward and prepares to turn.

2 The defender, trying to keep up with the attacker, is caught out by the Cruyff turn.

3 With the defender moving forward, the attacker is going back the other way.

4 The attacker has now created some space for himself and left his marker behind.

One-touch passing

No one can travel as fast on a football pitch as the ball. Swift, accurate passing will outpace the fittest and fastest of teams every single time. Effective one-touch passing is a difficult skill to master, but can be impossible to defend against.

Quick thinking and movement off the ball are essential elements. You must look up and assess your options as the ball approaches. Make up your mind where you are going to play the ball before it even reaches you.

Short and sharp

Your choice of pass will determine your success rate. Don't over-reach yourself. Keep it simple and within your range. Once you've laid the ball off, move into space where you can receive the ball again.

Coach says

- **Decide early who you are going to pass to.**
- **Don't be too ambitious. Short, sharp passes will cause the opposition as much trouble as long, high-risk passes.**
- **Weight your pass so it is easy for the receiver to control or run on to.**

Basics See the pass early

The basis of one-touch passing is pass and move. Be on your toes when the ball comes, spot your team-mates' runs and then make your passes count. When you've played your pass, run into space for a return ball. To keep ahead of the defenders, speed of thought and movement is vital.

Practice drill

Only two players are required for this exercise, designed to improve your feel for first-time passing.

Begin about 2m apart and play the ball back and forth, using either foot. Make sure you get the weight and direction of the pass correct. Then move further apart and take up a new position after playing each pass.

To begin with, stand about 2m apart and side-foot the ball back and forth gently. Keep your eyes on the ball.

Practise passing with the instep as well as the side of your foot – and remember to use both feet.

Once you have warmed up, repeat the exercise about 5m apart. When you have passed the ball, try moving off to take up another position.

Advanced Go through the middle man

For this drill you need at least four players. They form a circle about 20m in diameter with one player in the middle.

The middle man plays the ball to one of the other players who returns it first time to the middle man. He then picks out another player with a first-time pass.

The drill continues until 20 successful first-time passes have been made. Then introduce a new middle man. Once he has a feel for the drill, the middle man should attempt to move towards the ball slightly to make the pass early or allow the ball to run across him before playing it on.

Skills check

- Quick thinking
- Vision
- Accurate passing
- Intelligent, incisive running off the ball

1 As the ball comes to you, stay alert, on your toes and decide in advance which player you are going to pass to.

2 Play the pass first time. Don't overhit the ball or the receiver might have trouble controlling his return pass.

3 Having laid the ball off, think about where your next pass might go. Keep your passing precise and always stay ready.

The low, hard cross

When a player manages to outpace the opposition defence on the wing and is closing in on the byline, one of the best ways for him to create a dangerous situation in the box is by sending over a low, hard cross.

Adjust your technique

This cross gives the onrushing attackers in the penalty area a great opportunity to score and gets defenders in a tangle. The slightest touch – whether from an attacker or a defender – can send the ball flying into the net.

But for the cross to be effective, it has to be hit at the appropriate time. Crossing the ball low is useless if there is a defender between you and the penalty area. In this situation, you need to loft the cross so that it cannot be easily intercepted.

Coach says

- **Never lean back. Stay over the ball in order to keep it low.**
- **Always look up shortly before you cross and make your priority putting the ball beyond the reach of the keeper.**
- **Don't waste a good crossing position. Take your time and make sure you get the ball into the danger zone.**

Basics Cut it back

What makes the low, hard cross difficult to master is that it is usually performed while running at high speed towards the byline.

Get your foot right round the ball to cut it back into the danger area, just in front of the strikers. Try to get your head over the ball.

Don't rush the execution. If you do, you could finish with a slice off the outside of the boot, sending the cross harmlessly behind the goal or at the keeper.

1 **Get your head down, your arms out and keep your weight over the ball.**

2 **At the point of contact, wrap your foot around the ball to cross accurately.**

3 **Keep the follow through short. Then the cross will be low and hard for the keeper to reach.**

Practice drill

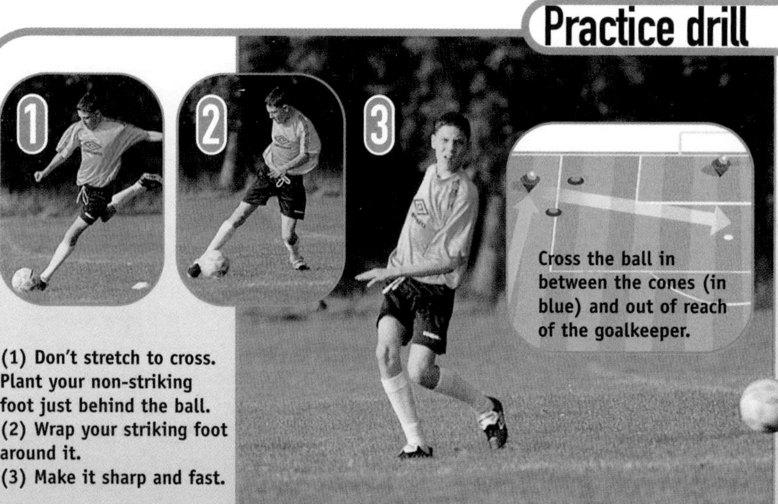

Cross the ball in between the cones (in blue) and out of reach of the goalkeeper.

(1) Don't stretch to cross. Plant your non-striking foot just behind the ball.
(2) Wrap your striking foot around it.
(3) Make it sharp and fast.

To improve the accuracy of your crosses, two cones are set 1m apart on the edge of the area.

Outfield players take it in turns to dribble down the wing and cross the ball between the two cones, directing the ball to the danger area between the penalty spot and the six-yard box.

Advanced Make it pay

Five attackers face five defenders in this match-play drill, played on half a pitch. The attackers also have a man on each wing patrolling a coned-off channel to provide low, hard crosses. No defenders are allowed in the channel, providing the wide players with space and time to deliver a quality ball in. The other attackers play the ball wide then must time their runs to meet the incoming crosses.

Skills check

- ○ Superb balance
- ○ Pinpoint accuracy
- ○ Excellent technique
- ○ Good power

1 Winger A crosses low towards the penalty spot.

2 Player B times his run better than his team-mates...

3 ...and tucks the opportunity away.

Spinning off

Tight marking puts space at a premium around the penalty box. But when defenders get too close, strikers have the chance to spin tightly round them and move into space before the marker has time to recover.

This explosive off-the-ball turn pulls even well organised defences out of shape. And if a team-mate spots the turn and plays in a through-ball, the results can be devastating.

Worth its weight in goals

The spin-off relies on the element of surprise, but your team-mates must be alive to your sudden movement, ready for the chance to play a through-ball. Timing the spin-off and the through-ball require practice, but the results are well worth the effort.

Coach says

- **Adopt a signal – a simple nod may be enough – to indicate to your team-mate in possession that you're about to spin off your marker.**
- **Even if your spin is not spotted by a team-mate, you will be causing problems for the opposition defenders.**

Basics Lose your marker

Perfecting the art of spinning is fine, but it will only pay dividends if you link with your team-mates. Practice is vital.

In this drill, a feeder at one end of a 20 x 10m area passes to one side of a team-mate, who moves in from the other end while being shadowed by a defender. The receiver uses his strength to spin off his marker, collect the ball and take it back to the end of the grid where he started.

1 Before the feeder plays the ball to the side, start your spin.

2 While you turn, keep your body between the ball and the defender.

3 After the ball has passed you, accelerate away from the defender.

Practice drill

Two attackers are marked by two defenders in a 20 x 15m grid. A feeder passes to one attacker, who either spins off his marker or plays a pass to the other attacker, who has spun around his marker.

The objective is to take the ball to the end of the grid. The second feeder can then start the drill again in the opposite direction. Practise spinning off both ways.

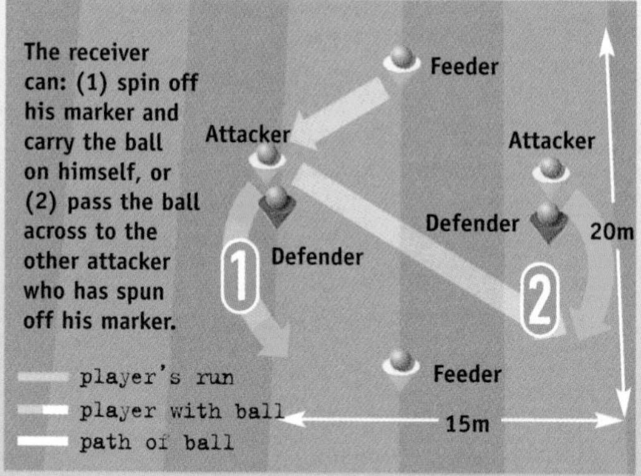

As the feeder plays the ball to one attacker...

...the other attacker looks to spin off his marker.

Advanced Go for a spin into space

Now set up a drill on half a pitch. Two feeders stand on the halfway line and play the ball to four attackers in front of them. They are up against four defenders and a keeper. The object of the drill is for the attackers to score a goal in a move that uses a spin-off.

Attackers should try to spin off into space even when the ball is not being played to them directly.

1 As the ball is played to another attacker, spin off your marker and burst clear.

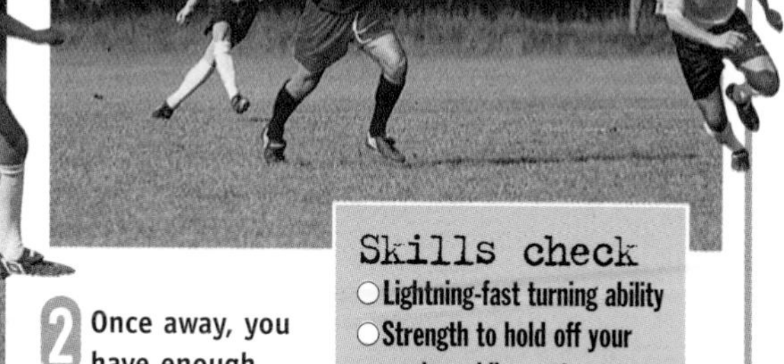

2 Once away, you have enough space to receive a pass or cross and head for goal.

Skills check

- Lightning-fast turning ability
- Strength to hold off your marker while you turn
- Balance and explosive pace
- Awareness
- Communication

The first-time shot

One skill common to all the world's best strikers is the ability to hit the ball first time. If a through-ball or cross is played to them, they don't need to take a touch to control the ball – they just let fire.

The beauty of hitting the ball straightaway is that it often catches the opposition unawares. The goalkeeper may not have time to get into the ideal position. He might not even be set to make a save. Likewise, covering defenders rarely have time to block the shot.

A test of technique

Using the correct technique is vital in first-time shooting. Even if the ball is bouncing awkwardly, a striker must be able to hit it powerfully and accurately.

Coach says

- **Practise with a moving ball – the ball will rarely be stationary when you want to hit a first-time shot in a match.**
- **Keep your eye on the ball at all times – don't lift your head to look at the target or you could miss-hit your shot.**

Basics Make a clean strike

Good technique is essential when hitting a first-time shot – your first touch on the ball has to be good enough to beat the keeper and score a goal.

To get your technique right, start by using a stationary ball. Concentrate on striking it through the centre and hitting the target. Then gradually increase the power of your shots – and remember to practise with both feet, so that you will not have to adjust your position in a match situation.

1 Approach the ball at a slight angle. Keep your head down and plant your non-kicking foot about 20cm from the ball.

2 With your eyes still fixed on the ball, strike firmly through it with your kicking foot. Concentrate on hitting the target.

3 The follow-through is every bit as important as the shot itself. Keep your head down and swing your leg forward and up.

Practice drill

The aim of this drill is to hit a first-time shot from a through-ball. The striker stands at the edge of the penalty area facing the goal. A feeder is five yards behind the striker and passes the ball forward at a variety of speeds and angles. Reacting quickly, the striker decides how to approach the ball to get the best angle and aims a first-time shot past the keeper.

1 The feeder decides to play the ball to the left of the striker.

2 As soon as he sees the ball, he sprints after it.

3 Without breaking stride, he hits a first-time shot at goal.

Advanced Shoot under pressure

This drill is played in the final third of a full-size pitch and involves seven players – a feeder on each wing, two strikers, two defenders and a keeper.

A feeder plays the ball into the box. The strikers must try to score with a first-time shot, timing their runs to beat the defenders to the ball. If the ball rebounds off the keeper or the woodwork, they should try to get in another first-time shot.

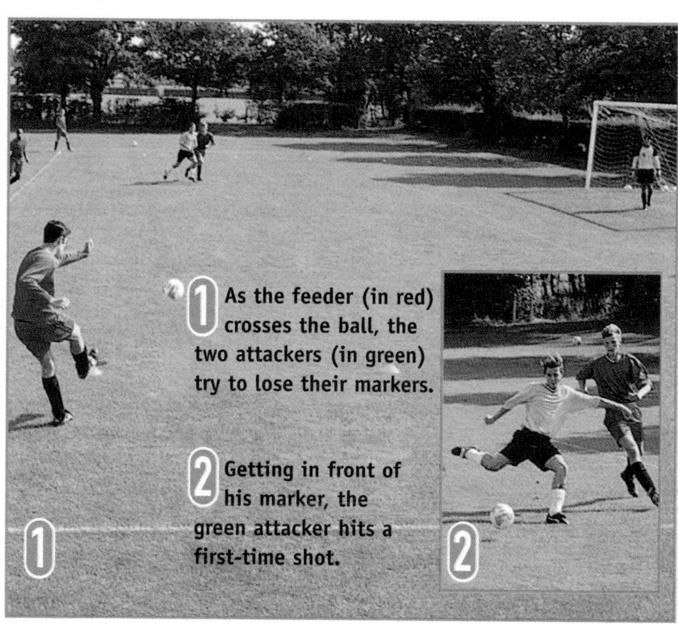

1 As the feeder (in red) crosses the ball, the two attackers (in green) try to lose their markers.

2 Getting in front of his marker, the green attacker hits a first-time shot.

Skills check

- Excellent positional sense
- Awareness
- Good shooting technique
- Eye for goal
- Ability to use both feet

The instep volley

Hitting the ball on the volley, before it bounces, is rarely the easiest option – but it is sometimes the best. If there's no time to control the ball, a volley may be the only way to strike on goal. A far-post cross, a headed clearance, a weak kick from the keeper all can be met on the volley with devastating effect.

Shape to shoot

Volleying requires timing, confidence and perfect technique. The slightest misjudgement and the shot can go anywhere.

Good body shape is essential. You have to decide early that a volley is on and get yourself in position. The rest is about the shooting basics – keeping your head down and your eyes on the ball as you shoot.

Coach says

- Get to the ball first.
- Position your whole body quickly.
- Get over the ball.
- Keep your arms out for balance.
- Strike cleanly through the ball.

Basics Make the right connection

There are two ways of making an instep volley – from the front and from the side. But the principle is similar. Try the first way to get used to the volley, then move on to the more complicated side volley.

Go forward to meet the ball and don't forget to follow through.

Skills check

- Speed of both thought and movement
- Determination and courage
- Good technique

1 Have a partner throw the ball to you at shin height. As you prepare to strike, straighten your foot by pointing your toes to keep the ball down.

2 Keep your eyes fixed on the ball as you make firm contact with your instep (laces). Use your arms to help keep your balance.

3 With your head still down, follow through with your kicking leg to maintain control of the speed and direction of the ball.

Practice drill

You will need three players for this drill. Player **A** feeds the ball – off the ground – to player **B**, who then has to volley it firmly and accurately back to him. Improve your accuracy by following through correctly in the direction you want the volley to go. Player **A** then feeds the ball to player **C**, who returns it the same way.

After 10 volleys each, switch roles so that another player becomes the feeder. Make sure you practise equally with both feet.

Advanced Take off, swivel and volley

When the ball is crossed from the wing, the volley is more difficult. You must hit it as you swivel 90° and you may need to jump to get over the ball.

For this exercise, a team-mate feeds you the ball from a line 10m away, at about chest height. Go towards it, adjusting your position as necessary. Keep your eye on the ball and strike it towards the goalkeeper.

1 As the ball comes over, take off from your non-kicking foot and rotate your body so that you face the goalkeeper. Keep your arms out to maintain your balance and keep your eye on the ball.

2 Strike over the ball to keep it down. A decent connection will produce a crisp shot at the target. Remember to break your fall safely by using your trailing arm.

The half-volley

Hitting a half-volley – when you strike the ball immediately after it bounces – is one of the most dramatic ways to shoot at goal. With practice, it is possible to get more power in your shot from a half-volley than from hitting a rolling or stationary ball. And you will be able to take the keeper by surprise.

Visionary shooting

To master the half-volley you must first learn how to anticipate the bounce of the ball at speed. Then you must position your body over the ball and remain balanced enough to hit it at exactly the right moment. Too early and you will strike over the top of the ball and scuff your shot. Too late and you will strike it with your shin and be unable to control your shot.

Coach says

- **Judge the bounce of the ball and react as quickly as you can. Don't attempt to hit the ball on the half-volley if it is easier to let it bounce up and hit it on the volley.**
- **Try to hit the ball with the top of your boot and follow the shot through.**

Basics Bounce and connect

Making clean, crisp contact with the ball just as it bounces is the most important aspect of the half-volley, as this is what enables you to get the extra momentum. To do this you need to perfect your timing.

Start by dropping the ball, letting it bounce and striking it with the top of your foot. Remember the basics of shooting – keep your head over the ball, raise your arms for balance and follow through with your shooting foot.

1 Keep your eyes on the ball as it drops and anticipate where the bounce will go.

2 Use your arms for balance, point your foot down and hit the ball just after it bounces.

3 Give your shot extra power and control by pushing your foot through the strike.

Practice drill

Stand 20m away From a team-mate and practise hitting a half-volley to each other, varying the distance between you.

Focus on directing your strike as accurately as possible to the receiver. Keep your foot pointing down and hit straight through the ball. Follow through along the intended line of your shot.

Controlling the power and direction of your shot will mean hitting the target more often in a match, and will make your half-volley very difficult for the keeper to deal with.

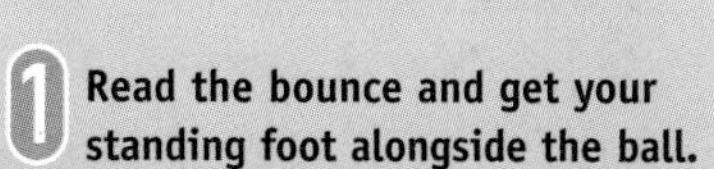

1 Read the bounce and get your standing foot alongside the ball.

2 Control the direction of your strike by following through.

Advanced Beat the keepers

1 The ball falls to the feet of the striker and he pounces to hit a half-volley.

2 Keeping his head over the ball, he hits it with power and accuracy.

Test your ability to hit a half-volley in a match situation. Three players per team play in a 20 x 20m zone with two goals.

Any player can pick up the ball, drop it in front of himself and hit a half-volley. He scores one point for a goal scored in this way. Two points are awarded if a player scores a half-volley from a team-mate's throw.

All players can use their hands to save the ball, so your half-volley must be well placed.

Skills check

- Agility
- Excellent timing
- Balance and co-ordination
- Smooth shooting technique

The long-range shot

One thing goalkeepers do not want to see is the ball breaking loose to players who have a good long-range shot. They know that soon the ball will be rocketing towards one of the four corners of their net.

The art of long-range shooting does not rely solely on power. The ability to strike the ball with control and on target is even more important.

Crack shots

What sets the world's best shooters apart is technique. Whether shooting first time or setting themselves up with a controlled first touch, they get into position quickly and strike smoothly through the ball, focusing on direction rather than power to send the ball past the keeper.

Coach says

- **Before you shoot, get your balance right.**
- **Relax when you are shooting. Try not to snatch at the ball.**
- **Know your shooting range – don't shoot if you are too far away from goal to trouble the keeper.**

Basics Stay balanced

First practise kicking a stationary ball about 20 yards from goal.

Don't try to hit the ball too hard – you'll lose your balance and the shot could end up anywhere.

Take a full stride up to the ball and concentrate on hitting through it cleanly and keeping the shot down. Controlled power is the key to long-range shooting. Eventually try to start aiming for the corners of the goal to make life difficult for the keeper.

1 The attacker strides up to the ball and stays fully-balanced.

2 He stays relaxed and focuses on striking cleanly through the ball.

3 He keeps his head down as he follows through smoothly.

Practice drill

1 The move starts with a crisp pass to the receiver.

2 The receiver lays the ball back into the attacker's path.

3 He checks his run so that he can take the ball in his stride.

4 He takes a touch to set up the shot and drills the ball home.

In this drill, two attackers combine on the edge of the box to set up a shooting chance.

The first striker plays a one-two with the second striker. He then takes a touch on the ball and hits a shot.

The emphasis here is on a good first touch and an accurate, clean strike on goal.

Advanced Take your chance

In this drill, defenders have the task of putting pressure on the attackers as they strike for goal.

The attacking side are given a six versus three advantage on a half-size pitch. They can only shoot from behind a line that is marked about 20 yards away from the goal.

With their extra numbers, the attacking side should always be able to lay the ball off to unmarked players for a shot. When an attacker is set up for a shot, he must react quickly, take a good first touch if necessary, and shoot before the defenders close him down.

Don't forget that the most important aspect of any shooting is to get it on target.

Skills check

- Confidence
- Composure
- Accuracy
- Technique
- Power

Despite the attentions of two defenders, the attacker is on to the chance quickly and gets his shot away

The dipping shot

The keeper is off his line as the ball bounces into your path within range of goal. Scoring is a possibility but you must stay calm and composed if you are to take advantage of the situation.

Learning to hit a dipping shot – one that rises and falls sharply over the keeper and into the net – gives you a vital addition to your striking armoury and the chance to score spectacular goals.

Why topspin is the key

The shot is struck on the volley or half-volley and uses topspin to make the ball suddenly dip. The topspin builds up pressure on top of the ball and drags away pressure beneath it. The ball dips because it is dragged to the area of low pressure.

Coach says

- Technique is the key when it comes to dipping your shot. Stay relaxed and let the ball flow off your boot.
- You can use the same technique for long passes, carrying the ball over the heads of defenders and into space for attackers.

Basics Hit it up and through

The key to getting the ball to dip lies in imparting topspin. To achieve this, you need to hit the ball forward and upward at the same time.

Get your foot under the ball and strike it hard with the 'laces' (along the top of your boot). As you do so, raise your leg and strike up through the ball to a high finish.

The technique is like an upward brushstroke – where you flex your wrist and finish with a flourish at the end.

Strike up and through to get the ball topspinning. It will fly high to begin with, then the topspin will bring it down sharply and under the bar.

Practice drill

1 Use your laces to strike through the back of the ball...

2 ...follow through as high as possible...

3 ...and stay relaxed throughout to ensure a fluid, easy motion.

This simple drill involves dropping the ball in front of you and hitting a dipping shot as it bounces up.

Lean back slightly as you strike the ball and then follow through as high as possible, bringing your foot up fast to impart the spin.

Your upward momentum may carry your standing foot off the ground.

Advanced Practise from shooting range

This drill takes place in a 30m-long area, with four players standing in a straight line at the 0m, 10m, 20m and 30m points.

The end players take turns hitting dipping shots to each other.

They drop the ball on the ground and strike it over the two defenders in the middle.

Skills check

- Good technique
- Awareness of the goalkeeper's position
- Shooting ability
- Composure

Drop the ball on the ground, hit it over...

..the first defender and dip it down over the second.

The curling shot

A long-range curling shot that bends around a goalkeeper and into the back of the net is one of the most satisfying sights to be seen in football.

Half of the battle in achieving success with a curling shot is confidence. You have to back your own ability and try your luck when the opportunity presents itself – the results can be spectacular.

With sufficient practice, you can master the skill and surprise even the best of goalkeepers.

Bend it in

A striker often uses the curling shot when he is faced with a defender between himself and the goal. In this instance, the only way to get a shot on target may be to curl the ball around the defender.

Coach says

- **Never be afraid to attempt the curling shot – you might surprise yourself.**
- **Your first priority is to hit the target, so concentrate on it.**
- **Curl your foot right around the ball to impart spin.**
- **The harder you hit the ball the more it will curve.**

Basics Swerve to succeed

In the diagram opposite, the striker finds his approach to goal blocked. But he spots the keeper slightly off his line and opts to attempt a curling shot into the far corner.

His aim is to bend the ball around both the defender and the goalkeeper, before they have time to react and adjust their positioning.

To get the curling shot right the striker needs the confidence in his spin to aim slightly wide of goal.

The red arrow shows the area of the ball to be struck to create spin. The striker demonstrates (right).

Skills check

- **Vision**
- **Confidence**
- **Good ball-striking ability**
- **Accuracy**

Technique Wrap your foot around the ball

1 Keep your head down as you approach the ball.

2 Use a high backswing on your striking leg as you move to hit the ball.

3 Always remember to follow through after striking smoothly.

Before you attempt to bend the ball around the keeper in a match, it is vital to perfect your technique. Before you strike the ball (from right to left in this example) put your arms out to help you balance and relax your upper body.

Use a high backlift, hit slightly to the right side of the ball and then follow through fully after hitting the ball.

Advanced Hit a moving ball

This shooting drill will help you perfect an accurate curling shot from distance. It will also help you deal with striking a moving ball. Outside the penalty area, the striker plays the ball to a team-mate, who lays the ball back into the path of the striker. The striker must attempt to hit his curling shot first-time. Timing is everything, so don't rush your shot. Set your sights just wide of the right-hand post. If you aim inside it, you will curl the ball too close to the keeper.

1 About 20 yards from goal, the striker plays a one-two with his team-mate.

2 Taking careful aim, he strikes cleanly through the right-hand side of the ball...

3 ...and his shot curls around the goalkeeper and into the back of the net.

Finishing at the far post

Your winger has beaten his man out wide and is shaping to cross the ball. You begin a looping run towards the far post. The ball comes over and you accelerate to meet it. How are you going to finish the move?

Make the decision

First of all you have to assess your chances of scoring – it might be better to pull the ball back across goal for a team-mate. Assess how much of the goal you have to aim at and how well positioned the keeper and defenders are.

If an opportunity is on, you have to decide whether you're going to go for a shot or header. If the ball is over thigh height, a header usually gives you more control and allows you to keep the ball on target.

Coach says

- **Always hit the target – even if the keeper saves, the rebound can fall to a team-mate.**
- **Watch the flight of the ball and make your decisions early. Then get to the ball and finish with plenty of confidence.**

Skills check

- **Athleticism and flexibility**
- **Good timing**
- **Quick decision-making**

Basics Practise your options

Deciding quickly how to finish a far-post cross is vital. Here, the striker shows three choices – the stooping header, the classic header and the shot.

For a ball over thigh height, it is easier to make a controlled contact with your head – rather than trying a high volley. Direct the ball low to the corners of the goal or hit it across the keeper – this means that if he parries it, the ball will probably be pushed back into the danger zone.

THE STOOPING HEADER
For a waist-high ball, the striker goes for a stooping header, so he can direct his strike.

THE CLASSIC HEADER
For a high ball, he goes for the classic header. He gets over the ball and powers it down.

THE SHOT
For a cross at about knee height, he elects to have a shot. He keeps his body over the ball.

Practice drill

Practise by passing the ball out from just outside the penalty area into the path of a winger as he runs. Watch the ball and run in to meet the winger's cross at the far post. The winger should vary his crosses – some hit high and some low, some hit hard and some flighted.

1 From the edge of the penalty box, the striker plays the ball out to the winger.

2 Before the ball returns to him, he prepares himself and decides how to meet it.

3 As the cross is low, the striker sidefoots the ball home with control and care.

Advanced Meet the cross

RUN TO THE FAR POST... The striker calls for the ball as he runs behind the defender.

...AND SCORE He races forward to head the ball home.

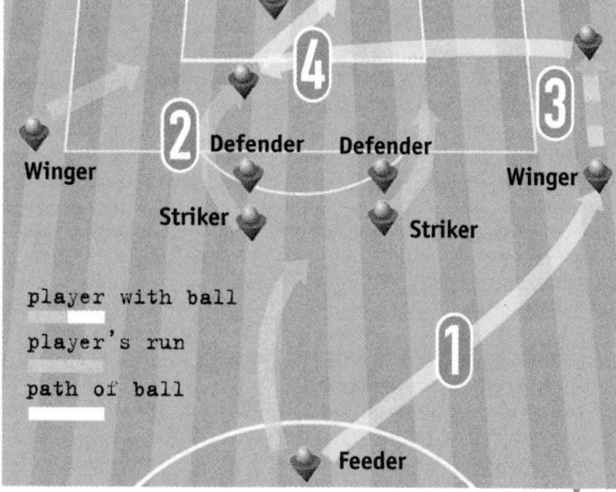

Now move on to a game using half a pitch, with five attackers against two defenders and a goalkeeper. One of the attackers plays the ball out wide for a winger to cross the ball to the far post. At least one attacker makes a run to the far post and attempts to score.

This drill works with the following steps. (1) A feeder plays the ball out to either of the two wingers. (2) The feeder, the two strikers and the other winger make runs into the box. (3) The winger takes the ball down the wing and crosses. (4) The ball reaches the far post for one of the attackers to finish.

The chip

A perfectly played chip adds a touch of grace and artistry to a football match. It may look easy, but it demands composure, balance and a delicate touch to execute precisely. The foot must meet the ball where the ball meets the ground in order to send it upwards and forwards.

Into the danger zone

The chip is often used as a pass, especially into the danger zone behind the defence. A midfielder may play a chip over an opposing full back to set a team-mate free on the wing or over an opposition centre back to an onrushing centre forward.

But it is in front of goal when the chip is most effective. If a keeper comes off his line, he narrows the target area to either side of him, but the striker has the chance to chip the ball over his head.

Coach says

- Use the chip for a pass only when there is a defender in your way or you want to set up a team-mate for a volley.
- A good chip will have a degree of backspin to it – so be aware that, as you make your run through, the ball will come back towards you.

Basics Use the lower instep

To play the chip shot successfully, you need to face the ball straight-on – in fact, it is almost impossible to chip it from side-on.

Bring your kicking foot down with a stabbing action – aiming for the bottom of the ball. Make contact with the lower part of the instep so that you punch the ball up into the air and follow through upwards with your knee.

Remember, the chip is about precision – not power. To perfect your accuracy, place cone markers at 10m, 15m and 20m away and practise chipping the ball on to them.

Use the lower part of your instep to get under the ball and loft it into the air.

1 Approach the ball in the normal way, with your head down and your non-kicking foot about 20cm inside the ball.

2 After you have hit the ball, check your follow-through so that the knee moves upwards rather than forwards.

Practice drill

Practise with a moving ball. A player passes the ball to a team-mate 10m away and runs towards him. The second player chips the ball over his oncoming team-mate and runs towards it. He passes the ball back to the first player, who chips it over him as the drill is repeated.

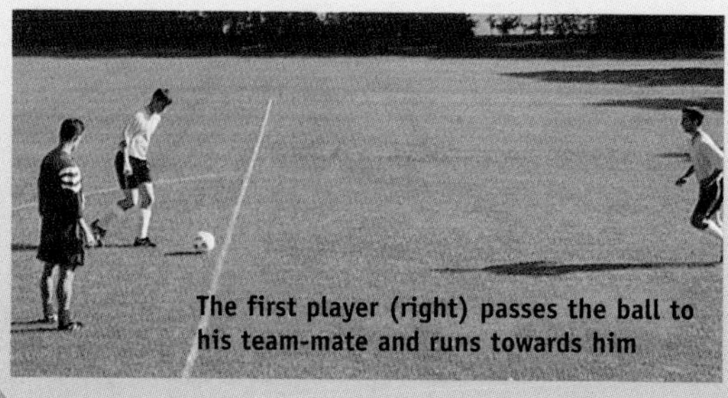

The first player (right) passes the ball to his team-mate and runs towards him

The second player chips the ban over the first player and then runs on to it

Advanced Chip and chase

This drill helps you to use the chip in a match situation. A line of defenders – with their backs to goal – are paired with a line of attackers. Each defender starts on the edge of the penalty box, and passes to his attacker 7m away.

Each attacker has to chip the defender, follow up the ball, then have a strike on goal. He needs to play the chip precisely – clear of the defender, but not so far that it runs on to the keeper. As the ball is likely to be spinning, the attacker may take a touch to control it before taking a shot.

Skills check

- Awareness
- Good composure
- Ability to deliver a controlled strike at the ball

1 The blue defender passes to an attacker and runs to him.

2 The green attacker chips the ball over the defender...

3 ...follows the ball into the penalty area...

4 ...and unleashes a first-time shot at goal.

The lob

A perfectly executed lob rates among the more spectacular sights in football. It takes good vision, sound judgement, great touch and a cool head.

Unlike a chip – which is played with the ball on the ground – a lob is played when the ball is bouncing. You can play a lobbed pass over a defender, but it is more commonly used for an attempt at goal. When the keeper has moved off his line, the easiest way of scoring is often to lob him.

A light touch

In this case, the player needs to be confident that he can not only lift the ball over the keeper's head, but also get it to drop under the crossbar. It demands a very deliberate, yet delicate, touch.

Coach says

- Keep your eye on the ball.
- Position your body early.
- Strike through with the instep to send the ball up and over.

Skills check

- Good vision
- Awareness
- Quick decision-making
- Coolness under pressure
- Good touch

Basics Strike through the ball

The lob demands great skill to achieve a controlled strike of the ball. When hit right, it should gain enough height to clear the keeper, but then drop rapidly to sneak in under the crossbar.

To get in a better position, stand on the toes of your non-kicking foot at the moment you strike through the ball.

And remember to follow through completely with your striking leg in order to control the direction and speed of the lob.

1 Keep your eyes firmly fixed on the ball as it bounces towards you and get your body in position.

2 Come up on to the toes of your non-kicking foot as you hit the ball.

3 With your arms out for balance, strike through the ball with your instep.

Practice drill

Get a team-mate to stand 10m away from you. Drop a ball in front of you and let it bounce once.

Before it bounces again, lob it up to your partner, aiming it over his head. Your team-mate then catches the ball and has his turn.

Practise varying your follow-through, and the strength with which you strike the ball, to see how its flight changes.

You can make the practice even harder by gradually increasing the distance from which you attempt to make the lob.

Be sure you practise the lob using both feet. During a match, you need to seize the opportunity to lob – even if it falls on your weaker foot.

Aim to drop the ball just over your partner's head.

Vary your follow-through to alter the ball's flight.

Advanced Work under pressure

In this advanced drill you can work on getting the lob right at speed. Two groups of two face each other 10m apart.

The first feeder (A) throws the ball to the first striker (B) and runs forwards. B lobs the ball over A to the next feeder (C). B keeps running forwards to stand behind C. Meanwhile, A has run across to stand behind the next striker (D) who then runs in to take his lob on a ball from C. The drill repeats as a cycle.

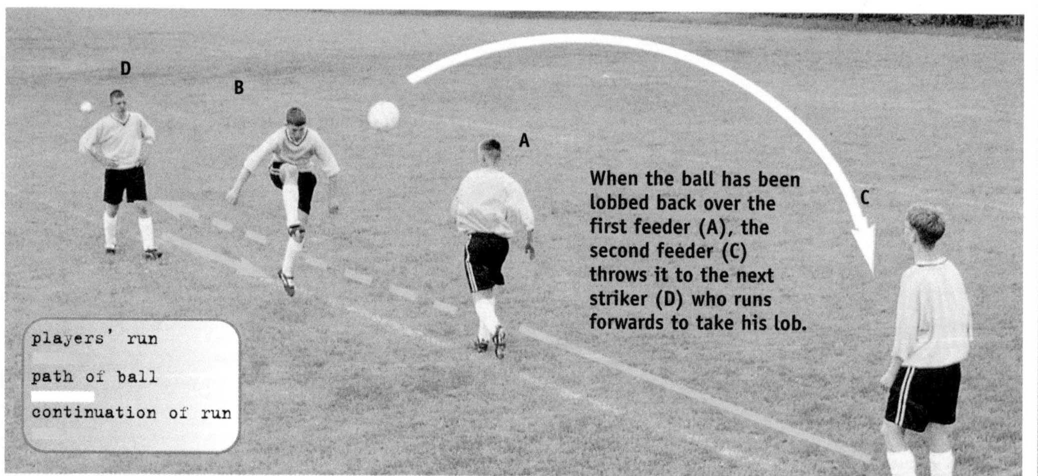

When the ball has been lobbed back over the first feeder (A), the second feeder (C) throws it to the next striker (D) who runs forwards to take his lob.

The overhead kick

When it is done successfully, the overhead – or bicycle – kick has to be the most dramatic skill in football. Of course, it is not easy. It demands athleticism and bravery – not to mention quick reactions and good kicking technique. But with practice, all players can master the art.

The advantage of the bicycle kick

The real beauty of the bicycle kick is that it turns a harmless-looking high ball into a goal-scoring opportunity. If a cross comes in behind you, the only way to get a strike in is to check, turn and try a bicycle kick. This will take the opposition defenders – and hopefully the goalkeeper – by surprise.

Coach says

- **Avoid dangerous play – don't attempt the overhead kick unless you are sure you have sufficient space around you.**
- **Use your hands and forearms to land safely.**
- **Keep your eyes on the ball.**
- **You'll rarely get a chance to perform an overhead kick – but when an opportunity does occur, make sure you're alert enough to take it.**

Basics Put safety first

The overhead kick has to be learnt in stages. Once you have mastered the landing technique safely, you will be more confident when launching yourself into the air. Practise the move on the ground without a ball, so that you can land without injuring your head, neck or back.

1 Bending forwards from the hips, with your knees bent and arms by your sides, lower yourself towards the ground.

2 As you start to roll, your aim is to ensure that your palms, and then your forearms, reach the ground before your back does.

3 Continuing your backwards movement, roll right on to your back and bring your leg up as you complete the kick.

Skills check

- **Confidence**
- **Agility**
- **Jumping ability**
- **Good kicking technique**

Practice drill

1 **Get a team-mate to throw the ball in to you. Take off from your kicking foot, thrusting your non-kicking leg up, to jump as high as possible.**

2 **Straighten your kicking leg and strike through the centre of the ball with your instep. At this point, your upper body should be horizontal and your eyes fixed on the ball.**

3 **Continuing your backwards movement, roll right on to your back and bring your leg up as you complete the kick.**

The next stage is to introduce a ball and practise the technique of using the overhead kick in the air.

Here, the attacker stands with his back to goal and a team-mate throws in the ball. Use a gym mat, an old mattress or even a pile of cushions, until you are confident you can land properly.

To strike the ball cleanly, your timing and co-ordination have to be absolutely spot-on.

Advanced Go for goal

Having learnt the basic technique of the overhead kick, you should now be ready to practise the move on the pitch in front of a goal.

Stand on the penalty spot with your back to the goal, and get your team mates to feed you balls as shown on the right. It is probably easiest for the feeders to throw the ball.

The overhead kick is usually an attacking skill but can also be used as a defensive clearance in the area if the ball is in the air and you are facing your own goal.

The feeders throw the ball to simulate these match situations: (1) A high cross from the wing; (2) A weak headed clearance by a defender; (3) A chip from a midfielder.

Attacking headers

Great headers of the ball make the technique look easy, but it is a very difficult skill to master. Headed goals require a good sense of timing. You need to judge your run so that you can connect with the ball with the right amount of force to guide, or power, it past the goalkeeper.

Making the commitment

Heading a ball for goal often means putting your head where a defender's boot or a goalkeeper's fist is likely to be, so courage is as important as good technique. If you don't go in with a degree of commitment, you won't present a threat to your opponents.

But once you have developed this skill, you will become a threat – from corners and other set plays, or whenever your team plays in a cross.

Coach says

- Time your run carefully, get away from your marker and attack the ball with confidence.
- With your eyes on the ball, head it downwards.

Skills check

- Quick acceleration
- Jumping ability
- Good heading technique
- Timing
- Courage

Basics Get your timing right

Good attacking heading is all about timing, but first you need to get the technique right. This can be achieved with just a little hard work. By following these three simple steps, you can learn the essential elements at home, either by heading it to a team-mate or against a wall.

Once you start to get a feel for timing your leap correctly and making firm contact with the ball, your confidence will soar.

1 As the ball is thrown to you – or you throw it for yourself – bend your knees and keep your shoulders square to where the ball will go.

2 As the ball comes to you, spring off one foot and time your jump so that you meet the ball firmly and squarely with your forehead.

3 Using your forehead nod through the ball and direct it downwards as powerfully as you can to the target, aiming for a corner of the goal.

Practice drill

Attacking heading is all about scoring. Add a goal and a team-mate as keeper to practise hitting the target. Get him to feed you the ball and try to score. Take five turns then swap over.

Work on your positioning. Get in another team-mate as feeder. Ask him to alter the position from which the ball comes to you. Swap everyone around after five turns each.

1 Attack the ball. Time your forward thrust to hit it with maximum power.

2 Keep your eyes on the ball, and try to aim it low and wide of the goalkeeper.

3 If you time it right, it will be difficult for him to get down to make a save.

Advanced Be first to the ball

The final thing to learn is how to lose your marker to get in a header on goal. Introduce a team-mate to act as defender and get another to deliver crosses from the side. Practise dropping off behind the defender to head high crosses and coming forwards ahead of him to meet low crosses.

Be prepared to dive to get in front of your marker and get a header in.

1

(1) As a low cross comes towards you, go forwards to meet it with your head. (2) Turn your body in the direction of the goal and meet the ball firmly with your forehead. Keep your eyes on it and try to control its direction. Keep your shot low.

Flick-on headers

The flick-on header is a potentially devastating attacking ploy which can take the opposition by surprise. It is normally used to lift the ball over defenders so that a striker can run on and collect it in a space. Many teams use a flick-on specialist for long throw-ins or on the near post for corners.

A flick-on consists of heading the ball on, either in the direction in which it is travelling or to the right or left.

Timing it right

The flick-on is most effective when used by a strike partnership. Both players need to have a good awareness of each other's intentions, particularly the striker who will be on the receiving end of the flick-on.

Coach says

- Get yourself between the ball and the defender.
- Jump early and as high as possible.
- Use your vision to head the ball into space for a team-mate to run on to.

Basics Keep the ball in the air

Get a team-mate to throw the ball to you in the air. Jump as high as you can, directing the ball on as it glances off your forehead.

The key to this move is to head the ball in the direction in which it is already moving, giving it enough boost to carry it over the defenders.

Skills check

- Awareness
- Determination
- Good timing
- Jumping ability
- Positional sense

1 Keep your eyes fixed firmly on the ball as it comes to you and get ready to jump for it at just the right moment.

2 Jump early and high striking the ball with your forehead when your jump reaches its highest point.

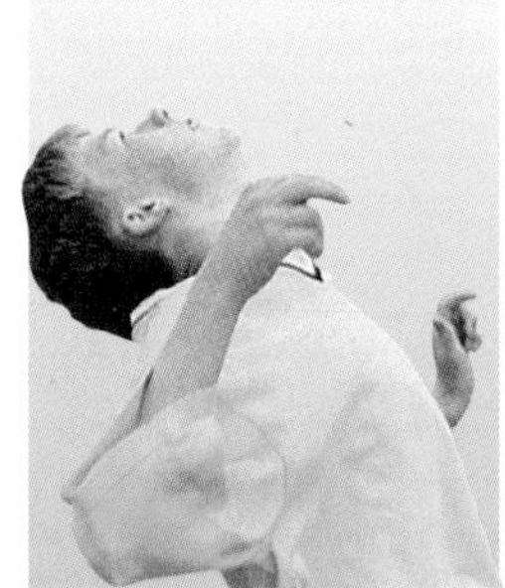

3 Let the ball glance of your forehead so that it keeps travelling in the same direction in which it was thrown.

Practice drill

For this drill you will need four players – a ball feeder, an attacker to do the flick-on, a defender and a receiving player to run on to the flick-on.

The feeder throws the ball in. As the ball comes towards the green attacker, he pulls away from the blue defender to meet it. The attacker jumps up and flicks it past the defender. The green receiver times his run so that he is in position to take the ball in his stride after it has been flicked on to him.

Advanced Redirect the flight of the ball

The feeder on the left throws the ball in to reach the attacker in the centre

The attacker re-directs the ball by moving his upper body and keeping his head at right angles

The feeder on the right receives the ball and throws it back, to repeat the drill in reverse

During a match, you will also need to change the direction of the ball with your head in order to find the space.

The same principles apply as before. You must come to meet the ball, jump early – ahead of the defender – and use your forehead to flick the ball on.

The main difference with the angled flick-on is that instead of the ball brushing off your forehead you must use your upper body to turn your head to redirect the flight of the ball.

Practise the drill above with your feet on the ground, then try jumping up to flick the ball on – both to the left and to the right. After five headers in each direction, swap positions.

Diving headers

All heading is about attacking the ball, but diving headers are the ultimate example. The whole body is committed to getting to the ball before a defender does. The reason? Diving headers turn half-chances into goals.

Put your weight behind it

Diving headers are powerful because they transfer the full weight and momentum of your body to the ball. They are extremely difficult for goalkeepers to stop, especially when they're targeted low down into the net.

When learning how to do diving headers, it is essential to follow the correct safety technique as well – so you can get up and carry on playing after you score!

Coach says

- Really launch yourself when you dive. A powerful take-off will add force to your header.
- Get your arms out in front of you to cushion your fall.

Skills check

- Good timing
- Confidence
- Courage
- Heading technique
- Landing technique

Basics Dive for glory

Diving headers are difficult, but with correct technique, good timing and lots of practice, you can learn to make them count without injuring yourself. Start slowly; have a partner throw the ball to you, fall forward with your arms out in front of you, head the ball and soften your landing by putting your hands down. Keep your eyes on the ball all the time and get your full weight behind it to power it towards your target.

1 Try to time your dive, keep your eye on the ball and take off confidently from one foot. Lead with your arms in front of you.

2 Head the top half of the ball with your forehead and try to aim the ball low. Drop your arms ready to cushion your fall.

3 Land with your hands in front of your chest. Avoid injury by relaxing your body as you hit the ground. Roll over if there's space.

Practice drill

The green player's team-mate (out of shot) has just thrown the ball in from the right.

The green player dives and heads the ball at goal.

This heading-and-throwing drill is played between two teams of four – three outfield players and a keeper – in a 30 x 20m area with two goals.

From the goal-line, the keeper throws the ball to a team-mate. He heads it on to the next player who catches it and throws it on for the third player to head. The team goes forward in this way without the ball hitting the floor or being intercepted, until a player can head at goal. A diving headed goal scores three points and a standing headed goal gets one.

Advanced Throw and dive

Two teams of two play in a 10 x 10m square with two goals in this advanced drill. Your partner throws the ball to you and you run and head it at the other goal. If an opposing team member catches the ball, he immediately throws it to his team-mate who heads it back towards your goal. If you catch it, you do the same back to them.

The idea is to keep the ball constantly moving. It's hard work – you'll soon find this drill is a good stamina test too. Again, you score three points for a diving headed goal, one for a standing headed goal. Don't forget to cushion your fall with your arms when doing the diving header.

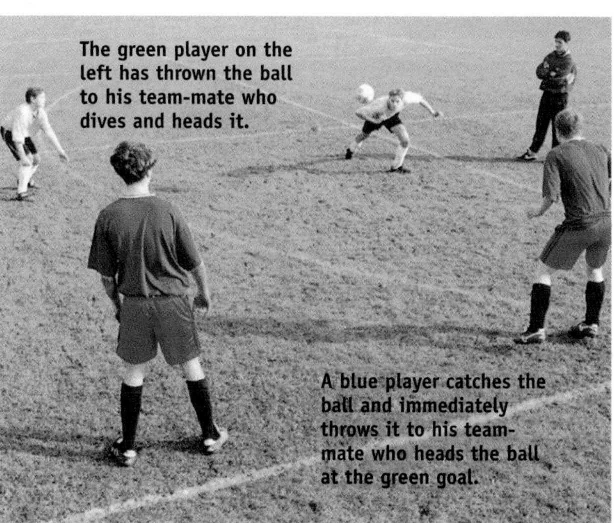

The green player on the left has thrown the ball to his team-mate who dives and heads it.

A blue player catches the ball and immediately throws it to his team-mate who heads the ball at the green goal.

Narrowing the angle

The term 'narrowing the angle' means reducing the amount of space the attacking player has to aim at when he is taking a shot at goal. It is the most important aspect of shot-stopping.

On the move

A goalkeeper has to know where he is in relation to the goal, and where the ball is, at all times. Good keepers move around the goal area constantly, so that they are in the right position to make a save. This positional sense narrows the target for the attacker.

Flying saves may be spectacular, but a keeper should aim to make shot-stopping as simple as possible – this is what narrowing the angle is all about.

Coach says

- **Position yourself between the ball and centre of the goal.**
- **Come off your line to limit the attacker's target area.**
- **Make yourself look as big as you can by standing tall with your arms out wide.**

Basics Get your bearings

Top goalkeepers concentrate on their positional play at all times, doing everything they can to minimise the area that the opposition can shoot at.

This is a simple positioning exercise. Side-step in an arc from one side of a goal to the other. Stay on your toes and keep in contact with the ground, so you can push off for a jump or a dive. Practise until you know where you are in relation to the goal without having to look behind.

In particular, be aware of where the centre of the goal is. To limit a striker's target area, stay in a direct line between the centre of the goal and the attacking player.

1 Stay on your toes as you side-step across the goal in an arc.

2 Move from just outside one post to the other. Return and repeat.

Practice drill

The goalkeeper should concentrate on footwork and balance, while trying to position himself in a direct line between the ball and the middle of the goal. His job is to make sure that the attacking player has as limited a view of the goal as possible.

For this exercise, two attacking players take turns to run with the ball into the penalty area and shoot at goal.

As each player advances towards the goal, the keeper comes off his line and spreads himself to narrow the angle. The striker shoots from a position roughly level with the penalty spot and the goalkeeper tries to keep the ball out of the net.

Advanced Come off the line

When an attacking player has a direct shooting opportunity, the keeper should always come off his line. This limits the area of the goal the striker has to aim at (see right).

Coming off the line is particularly important when a striker has a clear run on goal and is one-on-one with the keeper. Not only does it limit the striker's target area, it also puts him under pressure to shoot quickly.

And if the striker dallies on the ball too long, the goalkeeper may get close enough to him to close down his shooting chance completely – or even make a challenge on him.

Skills check
- ○ Quick footwork
- ○ Good balance
- ○ Confident judgement
- ○ Sound positioning

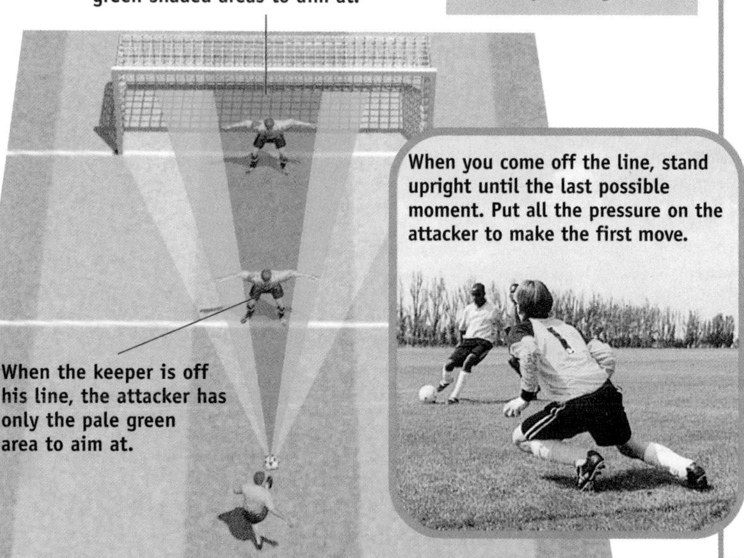

When the keeper stays on his line, the attacker has both blue and pale green shaded areas to aim at.

When the keeper is off his line, the attacker has only the pale green area to aim at.

When you come off the line, stand upright until the last possible moment. Put all the pressure on the attacker to make the first move.

Catching basics

Keepers have to catch the ball all the time – from shots, crosses and headers – and they have to hold on to it! Attackers are just waiting for the chance to pounce if the keeper spills the ball. Having 'safe hands' is mainly down to good technique.

Catch the ball in front of you so you can bring it safely in to your body. The key is getting into the 'ready position' before catching – head still, knees slightly bent, arms slightly spread at waist height, feet shoulder-width apart and weight on the balls of your feet. That way you will be perfectly balanced and ready for whatever comes.

Coach says

- **Spread your fingers.**
- **Watch the ball all the way into your body.**

Skills check

- **Good body positioning**
- **Correct hand shape**
- **Concentration**
- **Correct balance**

Basics Get ready then get up for it

Prepare to receive the ball by getting into the ready postion (below).

To catch high balls, bring your hands up into the 'W' shape: fingers spread, thumbs touching.

Arms slightly apart

Knees bent

Feet shoulder-width apart

Weight on the balls of your feet

1 Spring from your knees.

2 Pull the ball in to your body.

Practice drill

1 From the ready position, just collapse one leg under you when saving to the side.

Mark out a goal; one player shoots, the other saves. The shooter should aim some balls high, some low and some away from the keeper so he has to reach or dive. Let him get back in the ready position before taking each shot.

When diving low to your right, try trapping the ball with your left hand on top of the ball and your right hand at the side. This stops the ball from bouncing up and out of your hands. Reverse the position of your hands for diving low to the left.

2 Get your body behind the ball, catch it in front of you.

Advanced Get down to catch the low shots

1 From the ready position, go forward with your hands in an upside-down 'W'.

2 Scoop the ball into your chest to smother the pace and stop it bouncing.

To catch low balls coming towards you at speed, form your hands into an upside-down 'W': fingers spread with your little fingers touching. Go down from the ready position and scoop the ball in to your chest. If there's time, use the 'long barrier' kneel (right), which makes your body wider and keeps you stable.

The 'long barrier' kneel is a safe way to stop and gather low balls.

Turn one leg to the side. Get your hands in the upside-down 'W' shape and scoop the ball into your chest.

Fielding crosses

One of the hardest parts of the goalkeeper's job is dealing with crosses, sometimes called 'fielding'. Fielding crosses requires strength, bravery and good technique.

Keepers who regularly come off their line to field high balls are respected by defenders – for having the courage to challenge the attackers and for taking pressure off the back line.

Command the area

When a cross is played over, the keeper must judge the flight of the ball and decide whether he can get to it. If in any doubt, he should stay on his goal-line. Coming out and missing the ball will leave him hopelessly out of position.

If he is sure the ball is there for the taking, he should advance assertively, jump as strongly as possible and make a clean catch. Self-belief is vital.

Coach says

- If you're jumping to collect a cross from the left, always take off from your left leg, and vice versa.
- When fielding crosses, bring one knee up in front of you to protect yourself from on-rushing forwards.

Basics Catch it if you can

In this drill, the keeper practises catching the ball. A feeder throws the ball up in front of him from about 10m away. The keeper runs forward and claims the ball.

Learn to use the right 'body shape'. As you jump for the ball, drive off one leg and bring your other knee up for extra spring and protection. Get both hands to the ball, and catch it as high in its flight as you can.

1 As the player runs to catch the ball, he keeps his eye on it at all times so he can accurately judge the flight of the throw.

2 He judges his take-off point from the speed of the ball, then drives off one foot, raises his other knee and reaches for the ball.

3 Timing his leap, he gets both hands to the ball and claims it. He must then bring it into his chest and cling on to it as he lands.

Practice drill

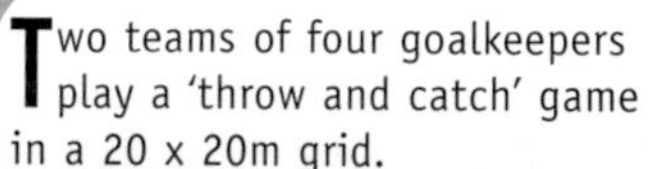

Two teams of four goalkeepers play a 'throw and catch' game in a 20 x 20m grid.

The object is to throw the ball to your team-mate above head height, while an opponent tries to intercept it. This puts the player fielding the high ball under pressure – he must attack the ball as strongly as possible.

Set a points target and award a point each time a team makes 10 successful catches in a row.

Skills check

- Quick decision-making
- Bravery
- Judgement of the ball's flight
- Powerful lift-off
- Good handling

A player in light blue throws the ball over head height to another keeper on his team.

Both keepers jump up for the ball but the light blue keeper gets there first and is able to claim it.

Advanced Make your mind up

In this drill, a keeper has to deal with high balls hit into the box by a feeder. He also has an outfield player challenging him for the ball. If he can't catch it cleanly, he should punch.

To punch successfully, make contact with the ball with the front of your closed fist. Use a powerful jabbing action of the arm to clear the ball a long way.

1 Face the direction of the cross and judge the flight of the ball.

2 Come for the ball decisively and choose to punch rather than catch.

3 Getting to the ball first, use a closed fist to punch it powerfully away.

Saving high shots

High shots can be a nightmare but can also give a goalkeeper the chance to cover himself with glory. Dealing with high shots is a matter of technique and preparation. Even if you're caught off your line, you can learn how to step backwards towards your goal while remaining balanced and ready to jump. It requires quick feet and quick thinking.

Don't be caught out

Certain golden rules apply: watch the ball and keep balanced. You will have to decide whether to catch the ball or tip it over. If you are well prepared, you'll be able to decide early and act positively – and you won't be caught out.

If the shot is slow, catch the ball safely in front of your body; otherwise, tip it over. When diving, take off from one foot to transfer as much of your sideways momentum as possible into an upward leap to give you greater height.

Coach says

- Don't panic. Set off towards goal using the crossover step to keep balanced.
- Decide whether to catch or tip. Be safe, not sorry.

Basics Catch or tip?

The pace of the ball helps you decide whether to catch or tip. Rising shots and slower shots can be caught. But with hard, swerving or dropping shots, catching is too risky. You might fall into the net holding the ball. Play it safe and tip it over the bar. Hold your arm rigid to block the ball and use the ball's pace to bounce it over.

Skills check

- Calmness
- Agility
- Co-ordination
- Quick decision-making
- Speed of reaction

CATCHING
Catch slower and lower shots. Form your hands into a 'W' to cup the ball, catch it in front of you and bring it into your body.

TIPPING
If the shot is high, fast, dipping or spinning, then block it. Keep your arm and hand rigid – the speed of the ball will carry it over.

Practice drill

The keeper runs back towards goal using the crossover step.

As he springs right, his left arm comes over to tip the ball.

Practise both the crossover step and tipping the ball over the bar. Start at the middle of the six-yard box and do the crossover step diagonally to both corners of the goal-mouth until you can tell where the goal is without looking.

First try the move without the ball, then get a team-mate to stand outside the penalty area and fire in shots at the top corners of the goal. Spring off the foot nearest to the goal. Your momentum should bring your trailing hand over the top to make the tip.

Technique Doing the crossover

If you're off your line, don't back-pedal to save a high shot. Do the crossover step – a sideways run that lets you see the ball.

1 The keeper spots danger and pushes off with his left foot towards goal, keeping his eye on the ball.

2 After planting his right foot, he puts his left foot in front. If he put it behind he would stumble.

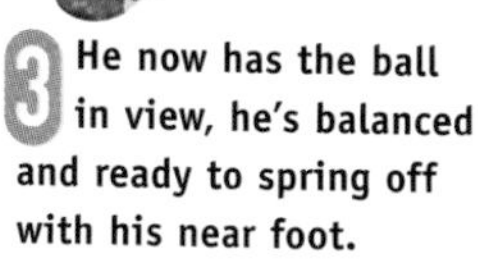

3 He now has the ball in view, he's balanced and ready to spring off with his near foot.

Reaction saves

The difference between an average goalkeeper and an excellent one can be a fraction of a second – the time it takes to react to a sudden shot on goal.

Remain on red alert

Whenever there is the slightest chance of a shot coming in, be alert and on your toes. Stand up in front of the attacker, with arms outstretched – but don't commit yourself before you know where the shot is going.

When the shot comes in, you can use any part of your body to save the ball. Ideally, you should get as much of your body behind it as possible. But if the ball bounces back into open play, make sure that you get back on your feet immediately. Ultimately, reaction saves are down to speed of movement – and the only way to improve this is by practice.

Coach says

- **Keep your mind focused on the game and be prepared for the unexpected.**
- **Be alert and ready to make a save from any angle.**
- **Stay on your feet until you know where the shot is going.**

Basics Take it in turns

A keeper often needs to make a save in a fraction of a second.

This two-player drill sharpens the keeper's reactions by limiting the time he has to prepare for a shot.

The keeper stands on the goal-line with his back to a striker standing six yards away. The striker calls 'turn' before each shot – the keeper then has to swivel and attempt a reaction save.

1 Facing his own goal, the keeper awaits the call of 'turn', at which point he must spin round, react to the shot and attempt to pounce on the ball.

2 On turning, take a step or two forward to make the goal as small as possible.

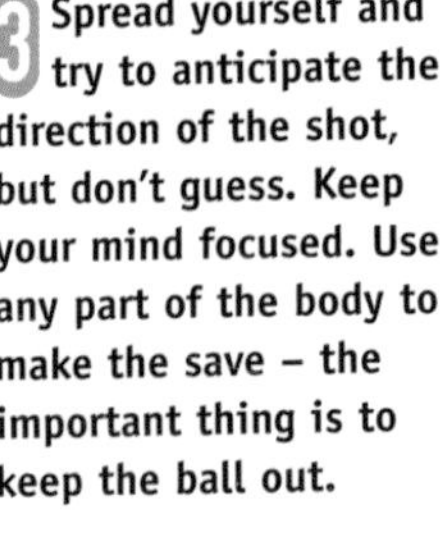

3 Spread yourself and try to anticipate the direction of the shot, but don't guess. Keep your mind focused. Use any part of the body to make the save – the important thing is to keep the ball out.

Practice drill

Now take this a stage further by lining up four strikers in an arc about five yards from goal. The feeder, who is inside the goal, rolls the ball quickly to any of the strikers.

The goalkeeper should be on his toes, with shoulders forward, knees bent and hands out, ready for a first-time shot from any of the four strikers.

Skills check

- Speed of thought
- Concentration
- Good positioning
- Fine footwork
- Agility and speed of movement

Advanced Sidestep into position

In this drill, a feeder stands on the byline about six yards from the keeper's near post. He passes the ball to one of three strikers in the penalty area, about 10 yards away from goal and five yards away from each other. The keeper starts at the near post and, when the ball has been played by the feeder, moves across to save a shot from the selected striker. Good footwork is essential – use small, rapid sidesteps to get into position quickly. Set your feet before you make the save.

1 The drill starts with the keeper at the near post.

2 As the ball is fed out, the keeper anticipates the angle of the shot.

3 When the striker lifts his leg to shoot, the keeper sets his feet and makes the save.

Diving basics

Diving is one of the most vital goalkeeping skills. The goal is 24 feet wide and eight feet high and the only way you are going to cover it all is by getting airborne. It's not good enough just to leap at the ball. If you use the right technique you can make sure your dives count. Anticipation, timing, technique, courage and leg power are key elements. Put them together to stop shots.

Safe saves

Diving is not dangerous, but you do need to take a few precautions. After making contact with the ball, relax your body before hitting the ground. Try to land on the fleshier parts of the anatomy – your thigh and the side of your torso and arm – rather than your knee or hip. Warm up thoroughly before trying diving drills or playing goalie in a match.

Coach says

- **When you dive for a high or wide shot, don't use a fist to tip the ball around the goal. The ball will bounce off at an unpredictable angle. Use an open hand and a strong wrist**
- **If you are right-handed, practise diving to your weaker, left side and vice versa.**

Basics Take off and land correctly

First practice diving saves in front of a full-size goal with a team-mate taking shots from 12 yards.

Only attempt to catch the ball if you are confident you can hold on to it. Otherwise, tip it over the bar or around the post. Try not to parry the ball back into open play.

Land on your side – not on your elbows, stomach or chest.

1 As you prepare to dive, thrust your leading arm away from your body. This pulls your whole body across the goal. Watch the ball.

2 Leap off your leading foot, bring your far arm over and stretch out. If you decide to catch the ball, form a 'W' shape with your hands (inset).

3 Once you have caught the ball, land on your side. Trap the ball against the ground with your top hand and then bring the ball into your body.

Practice drill

With really powerful shots, you often have no option but to parry the ball. In this case, you need to be up on your feet as quickly as possible, ready to deal with a second attempt.

This drill tests your ability not only to dive but also to recover and be in position to make another save.

Skills check
- Correct technique when taking off and landing
- Anticipation
- Courage
- Concentration

Mark out a triangle, with each side about 4m wide.

Three shooters stand about 2m from each of the sides, which serve as goals.

The keeper has to make a save from one shooter, then move across to the next side to save the next shot.

He moves around the triangle until he has made 10 saves.

Advanced Learn the 'collapse' technique

The shot hit low to the goalkeeper's side is one of the most difficult to deal with. Strikers often use this shot when one-on-one with a keeper, simply slotting the ball past his feet.

You may be able to block the ball with your legs – but remember, the ball will probably rebound into open play. The best answer is the 'collapse' dive.

1 Begin in the ready position with your legs apart and your arms out to your sides. Move down towards the ball.

2 Collapse on to the ball. Move your near leg across your body so you have room to get yourself behind the ball.

3 Trap the ball on the ground, with one hand on top of it to stop it bouncing. Bring the ball into your body.

Diving at feet

A striker is clean through with just the goalkeeper to beat. The forward looks sure to score. but the keeper comes out, dives at his feet and snatches up the ball. With a combination of timing. technique and bravery, the keeper has denied the opposition what looks like a certain goal.

Change the game

A great save like this can turn the course of a game. Not only has the keeper stopped a goal, he has given his team a psychological boost, increasing their confidence in their goalkeeper and defence. And diving at feet allows a keeper to dominate attackers and seem invincible.

Coach says

- **You have to be absolutely sure that you'll get the ball when diving at feet – otherwise you might concede a penalty.**
- **Don't panic. Stand your ground and pick your moment. The striker is under as much pressure as you are.**

Basics Go one-on-one with the striker

To practice diving at feet, get a team-mate to play one-on-one against you. He runs in on goal with the ball at his feet and tries to score, while you try to take the ball from him.

You should come out to meet the striker, not so far that he can chip over you, but far enough to narrow the angle – and confidently enough to make him hesitate. Pick your moment, then dive for the ball, collapsing one leg to get down more quickly. Dive to the side to present a longer barrier to the striker in case he manages to shoot at goal as you are diving.

1 Come out to narrow the angle. You should show confidence and remain balanced.

2 Pick your moment and collapse one leg under you in order to get down quickly.

3 Keep your eyes on the ball. Time your dive to steal the ball from the striker.

4 Get your hands on the ball and pull it in close to your body. You've saved it.

Practice drill

Many keepers prefer diving to one side more than another. This drill gets you used to diving both ways.

Two strikers are 1-2m away from the keeper at a 45° angle to him. Each has a ball at his feet, so that the keeper doesn't know which striker will run at him. Once a striker makes a move, the keeper must wait for a good opportunity, dive and pluck the ball from his feet.

The first striker runs the ball at the goal. As he loses control of the ball, the keeper dives at his feet.

The keeper makes the save – then gets to his feet ready to make another save from either striker. Keep the drill going at speed.

Technique Get your hand position right

When you reach for the ball on the ground, concentrate on getting your hand placement right. Your hands should be spread to form an effective barrier one hand behind the ball to stop its momentum and the other on top to prevent it bouncing out.

Grab the ball in front of your body, then pull it safely in to your chest, away from any onrushing attackers. This acts as another barrier to the ball's momentum. Keep your eyes on the ball and don't be hesitant as you go for it.

Skills check

- ○ Courage and confidence
- ○ Timing and judgement
- ○ Good balance
- ○ Decisiveness
- ○ Agility and speed
- ○ Concentration

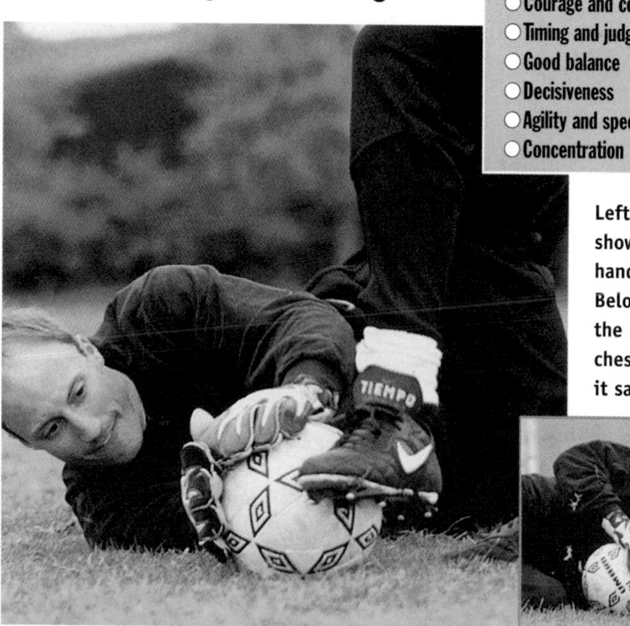

Left: The keeper shows the correct hand placement. Below: He pulls the ball to his chest to make it safe.

Part 2

TACTICS AND TEAMWORK

Learn the roles that you can play as an individual within your team and crush the opposition with devastating team moves.

The sweeper

A sweeper organises the defence. A defender without specific marking duties, he can cover and make interceptions where needed. He can also begin a counter-attack, make a penetrating pass or bring the ball upfield himself.

In the modern game, a sweeper has become the spare man in a line of three central defenders.

Skills check
- Ability to read the game
- Good communication
- Confident tackling
- Accurate passing
- Running with the ball

Basics Beat all attacks

The sweeper usually takes up a central position from where he can read an attacking move as it takes shape.

The example on the right, taken from a practice session, shows three situations. The sweeper, circled in the illustration, has to cover both sides of the penalty box and must act decisively to cut out any danger.

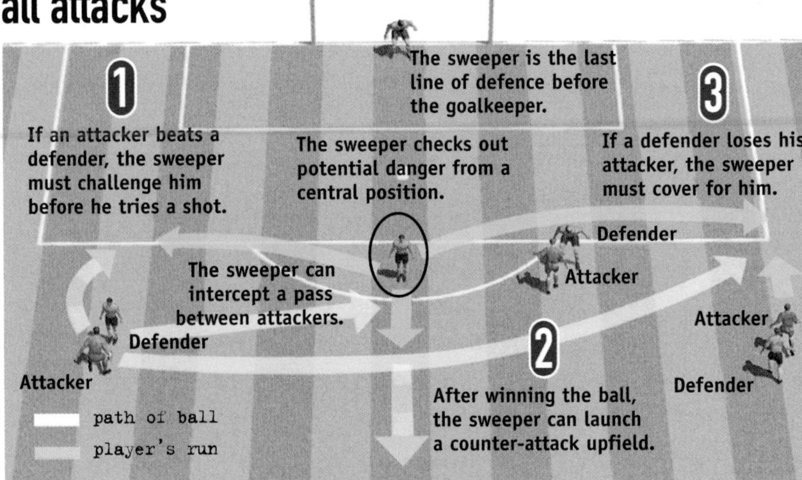

Practice drill

In this drill, the sweeper is responsible for organising his defence. Two attackers in blue play two defenders and a sweeper in orange. The sweeper calls out who makes a challenge on the attacker with the ball and who marks the other attacker.

If the attacker in possession beats his man, the sweeper must either make the challenge or send the marker to do it while he picks up the free man. Take turns in the sweeper role.

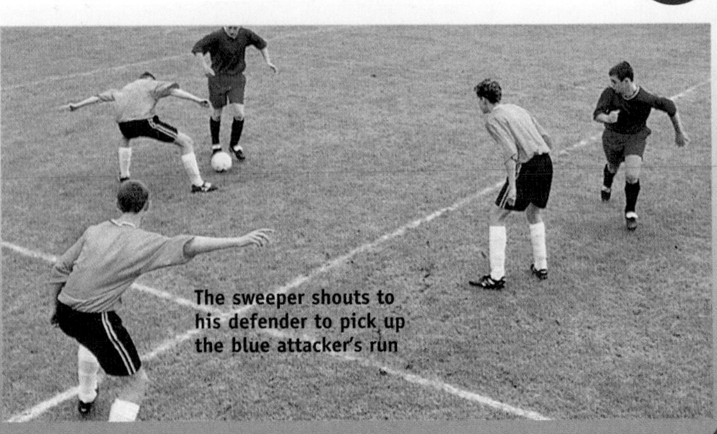

The sweeper shouts to his defender to pick up the blue attacker's run

The centre back

Much is expected of the centre back. He must be fit, tactically astute, quick in the tackle, dominant in the air and must protect his goal at all costs.

He also needs to be cool under pressure and assured in possession, bringing the ball out well or distributing it effectively. Often he is captain and leader on the pitch.

Skills check

- Strength in the air
- Confidence on the ground
- Good tactical knowledge
- Decisive and disciplined

Basics Take charge at crosses

Good centre backs come into their own when dealing with crosses. As the ball comes over, you need to make the right decision in an instant – whether to clear the ball or control it and pass it out of defence to create a counter-attack.

If in doubt, the safety first rule applies – clear the ball for a corner or a throw-in rather than risk it falling to an opponent.

For a cross, coming in from the by-line, you have three basic options. (1) If you are under pressure from a striker, clear the danger quickly and concede a corner. (2) If you get in before the attacker, clear the ball out to the side for a throw. (3) If you have some space, control the ball and find a team-mate.

If under pressure, try not to let the ball bounce before you deal with it.

Practice drill

CONTROL WITH FEET
If the ball comes in low and not too fast, control the ball with the side of your foot or thigh so that you can safely get it clear.

CONTROL WITH CHEST
Cushion a ball arriving at upper-body height on your chest. Relax your body as the ball hits your chest to bring it down.

HEADING OUT
With a high ball, head the danger away first time. Don't try to bring the ball down on to your feet – just clear it.

This drill helps the centre back cope with balls pumped in from downfield.

Three servers, 30m away, feed the ball into him at differing speeds and heights. Judging the flight of the ball, the centre back must decide whether to control or clear it. If you elect to control, be sure that you can 'kill' the ball instantly – otherwise, don't take a chance: clear it.

The full back

Fierce in the tackle, fleet of foot and swift on the turn, good full backs are an essential part of every team. They patrol the wide areas in a four-man defence, while two centre backs look after the middle.

The full back needs all his wits about him as he marks the opposition's winger or wide midfielder – usually a quick and tricky player.

Skills check
- Strong in the tackle
- Good positional sense
- Pace and turning ability
- Patience to challenge at the right moment

Basics Defend and attack

The full back's first priority is to defend. He must stop the opposition from making any headway down his side of the pitch.

However, whenever he sees the opportunity to attack he should take it. By making runs up the wing – with or without the ball – he will cause problems for the opposition defence.

player with ball
player's run
path of ball

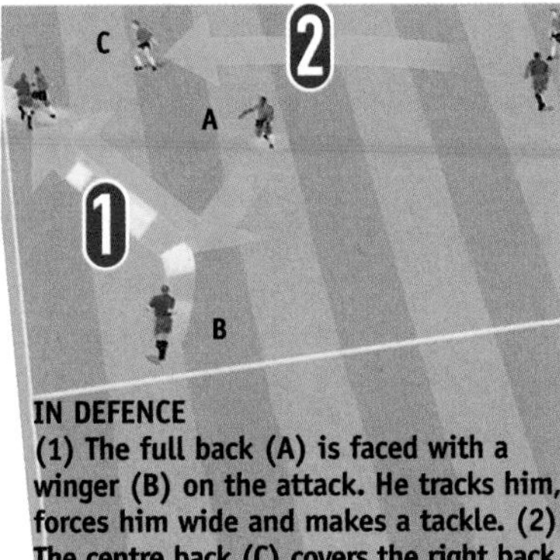

IN DEFENCE
(1) The full back (A) is faced with a winger (B) on the attack. He tracks him, forces him wide and makes a tackle. (2) The centre back (C) covers the right back.

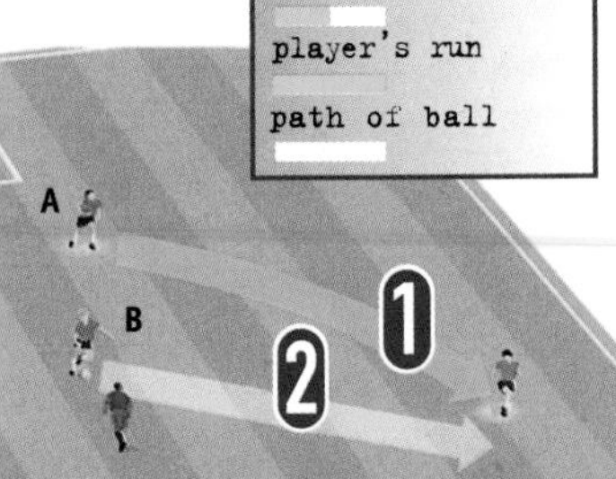

IN ATTACK
(1) The full back (A) sees the chance to run into space on the wing. (2) The midfielder (B) plays the ball to him and the attack is on.

Practice drill

In this drill on a half-pitch, a full back goes one-on-one with an attacker. Once the ball is fed to the attacker on the wing, the full back moves in to close him down. To control the situation, the full back should force the winger to go either inside or outside. Then he should track the winger's run and make a tackle if he gets a chance. It is helpful if the full back knows his opponent's game style.

1 The red full back closes down the winger and cuts off his route inside.

2 This leaves the winger with only one option – he is forced to go down the line.

3 The full back knows this so is ready to put on the pressure when the winger makes his move.

4 Using this advantage, the full back wins the race and gets in a well timed tackle.

The wing back

The term 'wing back' describes a wide midfielder who doubles up as a winger in attack and a full back in defence.

Wing backs play in midfield, unlike the traditional attacking full back, supporting the attack when possible, but tracking back as soon as the team loses possession. Wing backs need to be fit and fast.

Skills check
- Discipline in defence
- Flair for attack
- Timing of forward runs
- Great crossing ability
- Excellent fitness

Basics Learn to track back

This drill helps the wing back not only to pick up speed by running with the ball, but also to track back if possession is lost – defensive duties are a wing back's priority.

Use three players at one end of a 20m grid and a fourth opposite, with cones 5m inside each end marking the two 'lines' where players pass the ball on.

1 Player A goes on an attacking run with the ball. Player B chases after A for 15m – up to the far set of cone markers.

2 At the markers, player A passes the ball to player C, who sets off with it back across the grid to the other side.

3 Player A now touches the 20m line and chases player C – just as she would if she had lost the ball in a match.

4 C runs upfield, passes to D, touches the line and chases D back. Repeat until everyone has had two runs.

Practice drill

se this drill to hone the wing back's attacking kills. You need five layers – a midfielder and striker with the wing ack against a keeper and defender. The wing back egins the move by assing to a team-mate. he then runs down he wing, receives the all back, then crosses t. Take it in turns to e the wing back.

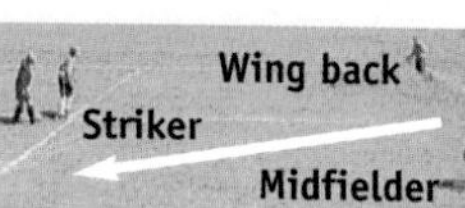

1 The orange wing back passes to the orange striker, who has a blue defender goalside of her.

2 The striker lays the ball off to the midfielder, as the wing back moves up the flank.

3 The midfielder plays the ball into the wing back's run, as the striker turns to run towards goal.

4 The wing back takes the ball in her stride upfield, while the striker and midfielder advance.

5 The wing back crosses the ball over into the box, giving the striker a good chance to shoot for goal.

The midfield engine

As the vital link between defence and attack, the midfield engine's job is twofold. He has to track back and help his defence – but once the ball is won, he must also support the attack. When there is a cross into the box, he will be there with the strikers.

All-round athleticism is required to fill such an important role.

Skills check

- Stamina to keep moving from box to box
- Strength in the tackle
- Willingness to track back
- Timing and awareness
- Good distribution

Basics Master all areas

Great midfield engines read the game well and tackle, pass and shoot with the best of them. But it's no use having all the skill in the world if you do not have the stamina – or desire – to back it up.

Players in this role must be as willing to get back and help the defence as they are to go for glory in attack.

Practice drill

Here, five reds take on two blues in the first of two 30 x 20m grids. The reds open the play so the engine can take the ball into the second grid. He plays a one-two with one of two reds at the end of the grid before running the ball back into the first grid and starting the drill again.

The midfield engine drives play into the second grid.

1 The reds work the ball so that the engine can carry it out of the first grid.

2 Once into the second grid the engine plays a one-two with either of the two players at the end of the grid.

3 The engine runs the ball back to the first grid, passes to a team-mate and the drill starts again.

20m

20m

30 m

The creative midfielder

Strikers may score the goals but it is the job of the creative midfielder, or playmaker, to make them. Every member of the team looks to him for inspiration.

As well as a great footballing brain, playmakers need all-round skills of the highest quality. They must stay calm amid furious midfield action and pass with accuracy and a delicate touch.

Skills check
- Intelligence, vision and imagination
- High all-round skill level
- Excellent awareness and distribution
- Confidence

Basics Create the opening

The creative midfielder must have the vision to spot an opening and the technique to exploit it. He should be aware of all the possibilities before receiving the ball in midfield but, from then on, with his head up to watch the play develop, he has to improvise. It is the unexpected that will open up a well organised defence. The playmaker is there to provide it.

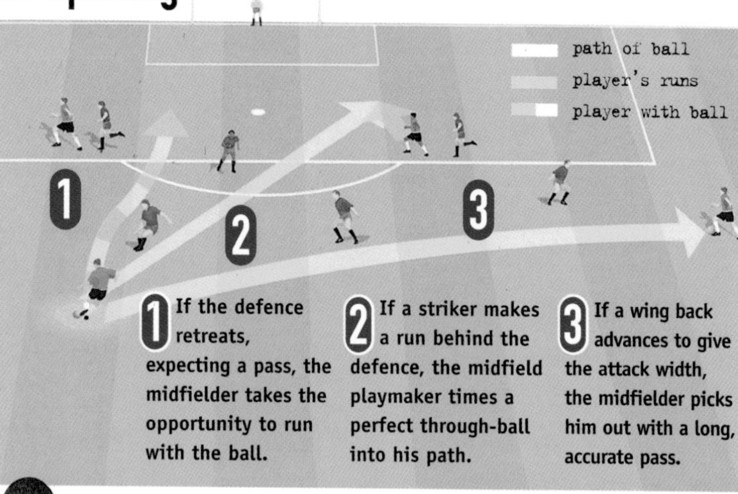

1 If the defence retreats, expecting a pass, the midfielder takes the opportunity to run with the ball.

2 If a striker makes a run behind the defence, the midfield playmaker times a perfect through-ball into his path.

3 If a wing back advances to give the attack width, the midfielder picks him out with a long, accurate pass.

1 Defenders hate midfielders running at them from deep. Each time a player is beaten, another gap in the defence opens up.

2 To make the defence-splitting pass work, you may need to indicate to your team-mates where you want them to run to receive the pass.

3 Switching the play to bring other players into the attack demands the creative midfielder to hit long, accurate passes with either foot.

The winger

Skills check
- Pressurising opponents
- Making runs
- Performance throughout a match

With his excellent ball control, pace and trickery, the winger in flight is a sight to behold. Nothing gets football fans on their feet quicker than seeing a winger bamboozle his marker, leave him rooted to the spot and cross the perfect ball for a grateful striker to put away.

The winger can beat defenders and deliver crosses, or cut inside and score.

Basics Stretch the defence

The winger's primary role is to provide ammunition for his marksmen. The usual way to do this is to take the ball down the wing and then put a cross into the penalty area.

However, good wingers can also create goalscoring chances for themselves. If they see an opportunity to cut inside, they can get into a position to have a strike at goal.

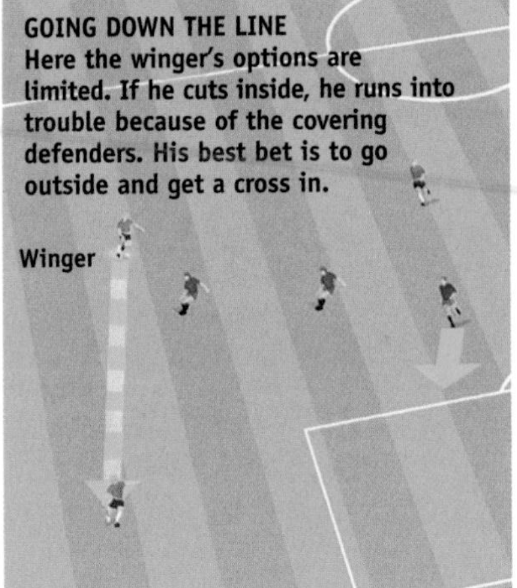

GOING DOWN THE LINE
Here the winger's options are limited. If he cuts inside, he runs into trouble because of the covering defenders. His best bet is to go outside and get a cross in.

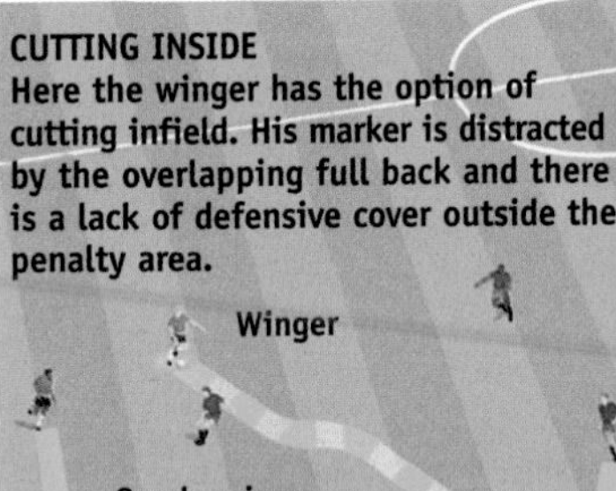

CUTTING INSIDE
Here the winger has the option of cutting infield. His marker is distracted by the overlapping full back and there is a lack of defensive cover outside the penalty area.

Practice drill

Set up this drill in the final third of the pitch to perfect the winger's skills at pace. Put some metal men or cones – representing defenders – diagonally to each other on one wing. The winger takes the ball between the obstacles at pace and crosses into the area, where two strikers and a keeper go for the ball.

Make sure the ball is under control as you weave between the obstacles.

Change direction swiftly to the outside and accelerate away, into position to cross.

When you get there, look up and concentrate on delivering a crisp cross.

The goal poacher

When the ball is in the penalty box, the goal poacher comes alive. He scores goals in any way he can, at whatever pace, height or angle the ball comes to him. His reading of the game allows him to get in exactly the right place and his heading and shooting ability, coupled with great reactions, enable him to make the most of every chance.

Skills check
- Surefire finishing
- Lightning reactions
- Speed and power
- Good reading of the game

Basics Be first to the ball

Speed of mind and body in the penalty area is the key to the goal poacher's art.

His intelligent reading of the game will take him into goalscoring positions or allow him to anticipate a rebound. Changes of pace will help him to lose his marker. And once he has a chance, he finishes quickly and accurately.

THE CROSS
The poacher (A) gets ahead of his marker to meet the incoming cross.

THE THROUGH-BALL
The poacher darts in to guide the ball low into the corner of the net.

THE REBOUND
A shot is blocked and the goal poacher reacts quickest to the rebound.

Practice drill

Striking the ball under pressure, with control and accuracy, is one of the most important aspects of the goal poacher's game.

In this simple drill, two feeders stand either side of the goalposts. The goal poacher stands on the penalty spot with his back to goal. One feeder then throws the ball towards him and shouts out 'Go!' The poacher must turn quickly, adjust to the position of the ball and try to score with either his feet or head.

1 When you hear the call 'Go!', turn on the spot and look for the ball.

2 Watch the ball, decide how to strike it and where you are aiming.

3 Make your strike as controlled, directed and clinical as possible.

Formations

Before 1870, when the rules of soccer were standardised, most teams played in a 2-8 formation, as there was no passing in the early game. The introduction of passing marked the start of modern football, and over the years a number of team formations developed.

The best formation

There is no such thing as an ideal formation. What works best for a team depends on what your strengths are and what kind of players are available. It may also depend on factors such as playing against a strong attacking team or even the weather conditions – heavy rain will mean you have to rely more on short passes.

Coach says

- **Don't overestimate the importance of formations. A good formation will help a good team, but skill and awareness count for more.**
- **Whatever your formation, communication is vital. Keep in touch with your team-mates in all positions.**
- **Be prepared to change your formation as the match progresses.**

Basics 4-4-2

The 4-4-2 formation is probably the most common one in the modern game, with a good balance throughout the positions. Four defenders and four midfielders mean it's a solid system that can be used when playing against strong opposition. But it can also be an effective attacking formation, especially if you have two strong forwards who can outrun the opposition defence and fast, attacking midfielders who can bring the ball upfield.

Advanced 3-5-2

This formation is more attacking than 4-4-2 and is best with an experienced team who are good communicators throughout the pitch. With only three at the back, defenders must be solid and work together as a unit. They must also communicate well with the midfield, since midfielders may often be called upon to take a defensive role. When defending, one forward will often drop back in support. In attacking play, this system often depends on an intelligent and skilful central midfielder who can read the game and link up with the forwards.

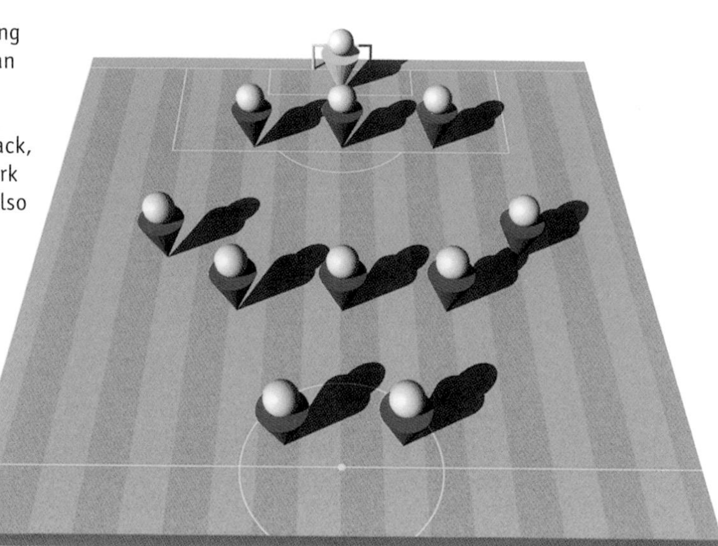

Advanced 4-5-1

The 4-5-1 formation is hardly ever used as a starting lineup. It's most often used to protect a lead late on in the game. With a packed midfield, it's good for holding the ball. Central midfielders can use short passes to keep possession and even link up with the lone forward, though he will have a lot of work to do and is unlikely to get many scoring chances. Wing-backs can also be used to bring the ball out of defence. This formation can be used either with a sweeper or with a flat back four.

The offside law

In defence or attack, knowing and using the offside law will improve your team's performance. If a player is offside, the referee will award an indirect free kick to the other team from the place where the infringement occurred.

Caught offside

To be offside, you must have fewer than two opposition players between yourself and the goal-line at the moment the ball is played to you. You must be between the goal-line and the ball and you must be inside the opposition half. The only exceptions are when your team-mate throws or passes the ball directly to you from a goal-kick, corner-kick or throw-in. In all these cases, you cannot be offside.

Coach says

- The law is designed to stop players goalhanging – seeking scoring chances by standing behind the opposition defence.
- Learn the offside law. Don't let your ignorance prevent a goal or gift one to the opposition.
- If the keeper is stranded upfield and you only have an outfield player between you and the goal, you are still offside.

Basics Being offside

When a player passes the ball up the field, the referee and his assistants check the positions of the player's attacking team-mates relative to the opposition defence and goalkeeper.

The diagram opposite shows how the positions of attacking players when a ball is played forward can lead to a referee ruling them on or offside.

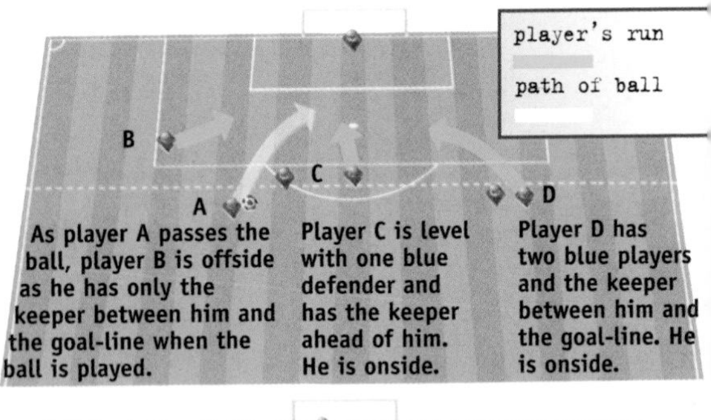

As player A passes the ball, player B is offside as he has only the keeper between him and the goal-line when the ball is played. Player C is level with one blue defender and has the keeper ahead of him. He is onside. Player D has two blue players and the keeper between him and the goal-line. He is onside.

Interfering with play

Being in an offside position does not mean that the referee will automatically stop play. He must decide whether you are also interfering with play.

To do this he imagines a zone (here in orange) inside which you would normally be judged as interfering. This helps him make the decision.

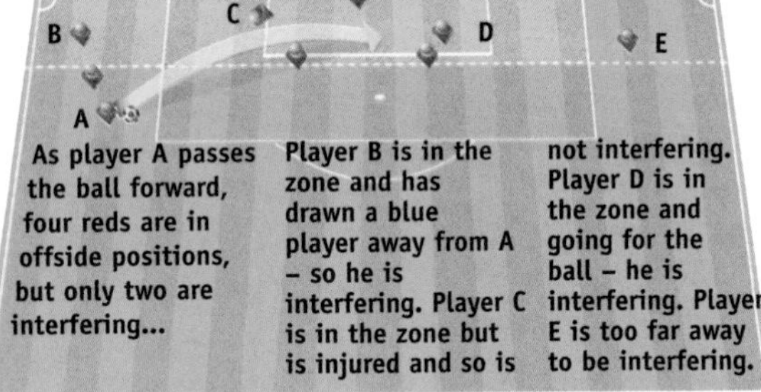

As player A passes the ball forward, four reds are in offside positions, but only two are interfering... Player B is in the zone and has drawn a blue player away from A – so he is interfering. Player C is in the zone but is injured and so is not interfering. Player D is in the zone and going for the ball – he is interfering. Player E is too far away to be interfering.

Coach's recap

The offside law can seem difficult to understand, but by learning these six rules you can use the law to your advantage. Defenders can learn the offside trap and attackers can learn how to beat it.

The offside trap is where a defender or, more often, a defensive unit acting on a signal, rush forward in order to catch an attacking player offside. Alert attackers will be on the lookout for this ploy.

1 Your position will be judged at the moment the ball is passed.
2 If you have one opponent – or none – between you and the goal-line, you are offside. But you are onside if you have one opponent in front of you and you are level with the second to last opposing player.
3 You can only be offside if you are in front of the ball when it is played forward.
4 You cannot be offside directly from a throw-in, corner or goal-kick. But as soon as another of your players touches the ball the offside rule can be applied.
5 You cannot be offside if you are inside your own half.
6 If you are offside, the referee gives an indirect free kick to the opposition.

The offside trap

One of the most effective ways for a defence to stop an attack is by setting an offside trap. When a forward ball is played, an attacker who is caught between the last defender and the goalkeeper is offside. Defenders set the trap by playing in a line across the pitch and running forward as a unit, perhaps on a signal. The tactic leaves unwary attackers stranded offside.

Dangerous play

The offside trap can be risky. Communication and anticipation are vital. All the defenders have to time their runs so that they move past the attackers before the ball is played. If even one defender is slow off the mark, the consequences can be disastrous. If a striker is level with the last defender, he's onside and can run on to the pass unchallenged.

Coach says

- **Anticipation is the key. At the moment the pass is struck to the attacker, all the defenders must already be ahead of him.**
- **Even if you're going to adopt an offside trap, don't forget to defend. If you can reach the ball, clear it. That's the safe option: the offside trap isn't, but it's a useful fall-back.**

Basics Hold your line

The offside trap relies on speed and surprise. When a striker is poised and waiting for a pass, he will expect defenders to be goalside of him and he'll be watching the passer, not the defence.

It's essential for the defence to hold the line – constantly checking their positions against each other – and step forward together at the right moment. They must move up as a unit, holding the line as they go.

The red defenders set the offside trap by holding a line about 10 yards in front of their own penalty box. Anticipating attacker A's pass, they spring the trap by stepping up in a line before the ball is played. Player B is left stranded offside.

Skills check

- **Communication**
- **Teamwork**
- **Timing**
- **Speed**

Practice drill

In a 40 x 40m square, three attackers face three defenders and a keeper. Two feeders near the 40m line pass the ball up to the attackers, varying the pace and direction of their deliveries. The defenders must spring the offside trap in unison – without forgetting to defend their goal.

1 The red defenders try to hold a line against the blue attackers, who are all clearly onside.

2 Just before the pass is played, the defenders spring the trap by running forward as a unit.

3 By the time the ball is played through, the two far attackers have been caught offside.

Advanced Beating the offside trap

To beat the offside trap, attackers must have pace, awareness and timing. Movement off the ball is crucial; attackers who stand still are not only easy to mark, they also get caught offside. Players will often make diagonal runs to stay onside, then dart through to meet a pass. In the examples below, the attackers are aware of the defenders' positions and move the ball swiftly to outwit them.

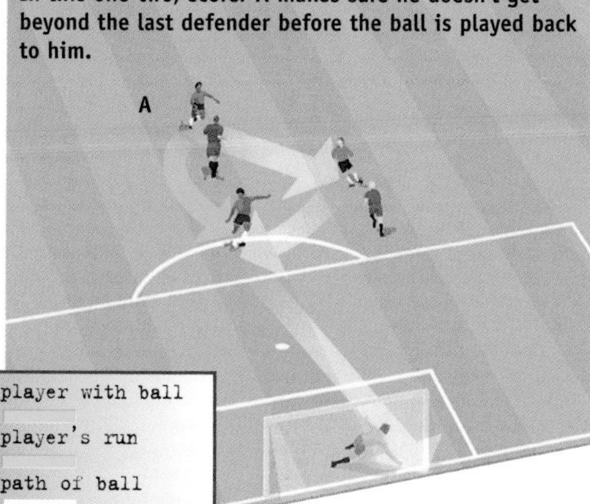

In this one-two, scorer A makes sure he doesn't get beyond the last defender before the ball is played back to him.

Here scorer B uses an angled run. He begins a run parallel to the defensive line (1), waits until the ball is played, then darts inside (2).

Defending as a unit

The world's best defenders are forever talking. They know the positions of their team-mates, the opposition and the ball. This means they can read situations as – or before – they develop and react accordingly.

Above all else, they are organised and disciplined: they work as a unit. Translated on to the pitch, this means they never leave a defender one-on-one with an attacker. There is always cover.

Covering up

So when a four-man defence plays against a two-man attack, two of the defenders mark the attackers while the other two provide cover. If one of the attackers beats his man, then he has another defender to cope with.

Coach says

- **Always close down the player with the ball first. The next closest defender should then provide cover.**
- **Force the ball backwards or sideways. Get it away from the dangerous central areas and out to the wings.**

Basics Defend in depth

To defend successfully, players should cover each other by lining up in a staggered formation – some players standing deeper than others.

In this way the deeper defenders can deal with a through-ball or a ball over the top, and also provide cover for the other defenders. If an attacker beats the first tackle, the defence should make sure he runs into another one. If the attacker passes the ball square, a defender should then pressurise the receiver.

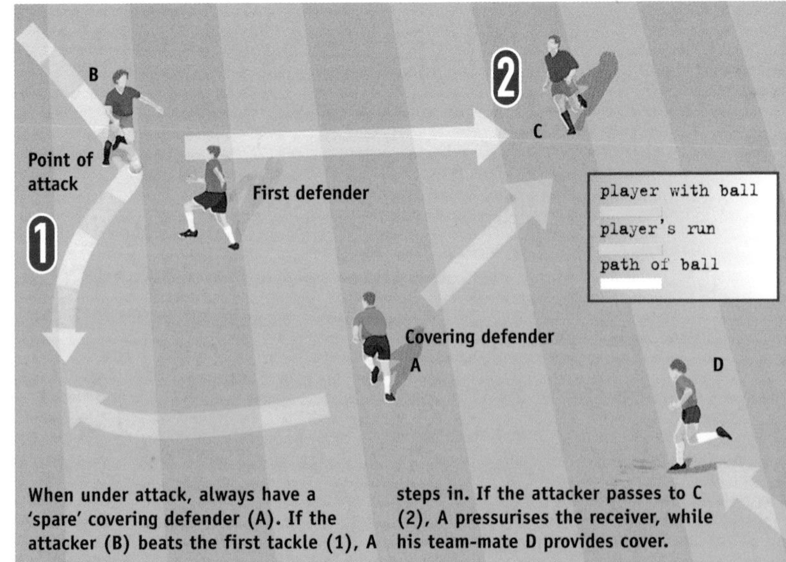

When under attack, always have a 'spare' covering defender (A). If the attacker (B) beats the first tackle (1), A steps in. If the attacker passes to C (2), A pressurises the receiver, while his team-mate D provides cover.

Practice drill

On a 10 x 20m grid with a small goal at either end, two players apply the basics of defending as a unit against two forwards. Their aim is to stop the attack and then move upfield in a counter-attack of their own. They should communicate constantly and cover each other.

Skills check
- Good communication
- Positional sense
- Concentration

1 In this fine defensive stance, one player pressurises the man on the ball, the other provides good cover.

2 When the second attacker moves in, the covering defender closes him down, while his partner drops off.

3 Communicating well, the defence have the situation in hand and the attacker is forced into a mistake.

Advanced Close down and cover

The drill is expanded to four against four on a 20 x 30m grid. With more possible points of attack, the defenders must offer each other positional advice, talking to each other to ensure that they are lined up in an effective formation to deal with the situation.

One defender should pressurise the attacker with the ball. If possible, he should force him down the wing, away from goal.

The reds offer classic diagonal defensive cover inside and force the blue attacker out to the wing.

One defender confronts the attacker, while another covers nearby, limiting the striker's options for moving up the pitch.

Man-to-man marking

There are two basic methods of defending: a zonal system and man-to-man marking. In using a zonal system, defenders pick up any opponent who enters a given area on the pitch. But in a man-marking system, each defender takes on the responsibility for marking one of the opposing team.

Individual responsibility

All the skills of marking come into play: staying goalside, keeping close to the player you are marking, trying to intercept passes to or from him, pressuring him when he does get the ball and robbing him of possession whenever you get the chance.

Coach says

- Always keep goalside.
- Make a point of anticipating your opponent's next move.
- Good interception can help lead to an immediate counter-attack for your side.

Basics Stick to the same opponent

The aim for any defender or midfielder who is man-marking his opponent is straightforward: NEVER leave your player's side. Get yourself between the ball and the goal, and deny him space in which he can turn with the ball or score with it.

If your opponent makes a run, you must cover the movement. This takes maximum concentration, good vision, speed, and determination – as well as a high level of fitness and stamina.

Practice drill

Three blue players with a ball each stand outside a 10 x 10m square. A blue attacker and an orange defender stay inside. The attacker calls for a ball and the defender man-marks him tightly to stop him scoring at the free edge of the square. Take five turns each to play the man-marker.

The marker stays close and makes it hard for the attacker to play the ball

The blue attacker can call for a pass from any of the other blue players. The orange player must defend the free edge of the square and stop the attacker scoring.

Skills check

- Ability to turn quickly
- Effective positioning
- Concentration
- Communication
- Pace
- Tackling ability
- High level of fitness

Basics Work the tactics onto the pitch

Two teams of five players practise on a 40 x 30m pitch, using small goals and no keepers. Every player has one partner from the opposing team. He is the only one who can tackle that player and vice versa. Drills of 10 minutes each side will teach the team the various skills of man-marking, as well as develop good tactical habits.

This defender can frustrate shots by staying goalside.

This defender is goalside of the ball but can still close down his opponent.

This marker is in a good position but not close enough to intercept a forward pass.

This player is now free to receive a backward pass.

Hunting in packs

Good teamwork comes from understanding, communication and hard work. Hunting in packs demands all three. This pressurising defensive strategy is the job of the midfield. They condense the play and deny the opposition time and space to develop attacks by swarming around the player with the ball to dispossess him.

Defend as a unit

One player challenges the ball carrier. He closes him down and tries to tackle. He is supported by another player and the rest of the midfield pack. They close in on the ball, while the defence marks tightly to shut down passing options. The pack anticipates and reacts when the ball breaks loose, then clean up and counter-attack.

Coach says

- **Support the tackler. Alone, he can be easily passed by.**
- **Anticipate. Be ready to intercept the ball.**
- **Get your tackle in.**

Practice drill

Three defenders must work even harder as a unit to win possession from six attackers in the continuous drill below. The six blues start by passing the ball around in the left half of the grid. Three of the reds have to hunt as a pack to win the ball from them. Only then can they pass it to the three reds standing waiting in the other half and cross the line to join them. They now become the attacking team. Three of the blues cross over to become defenders and the drill starts over again.

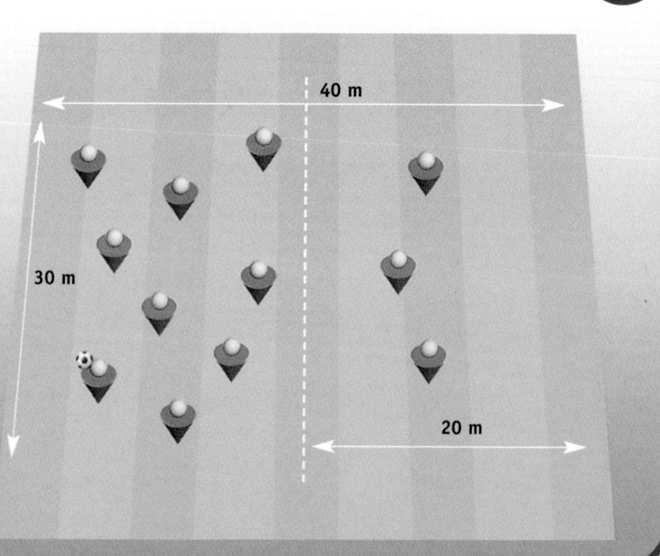

Basics Close in to win the ball

Teams that hunt in packs have to work as a unit (right). As players near to the ball-carrier move in to tackle and dispossess him, the rest of the team must mark tightly to smother his passing options.

In the drill below, six blue attackers play four red defenders in a 40 x 40m square with no goals. The blues try to keep the ball; the reds must hunt in a pack to dispossess them.

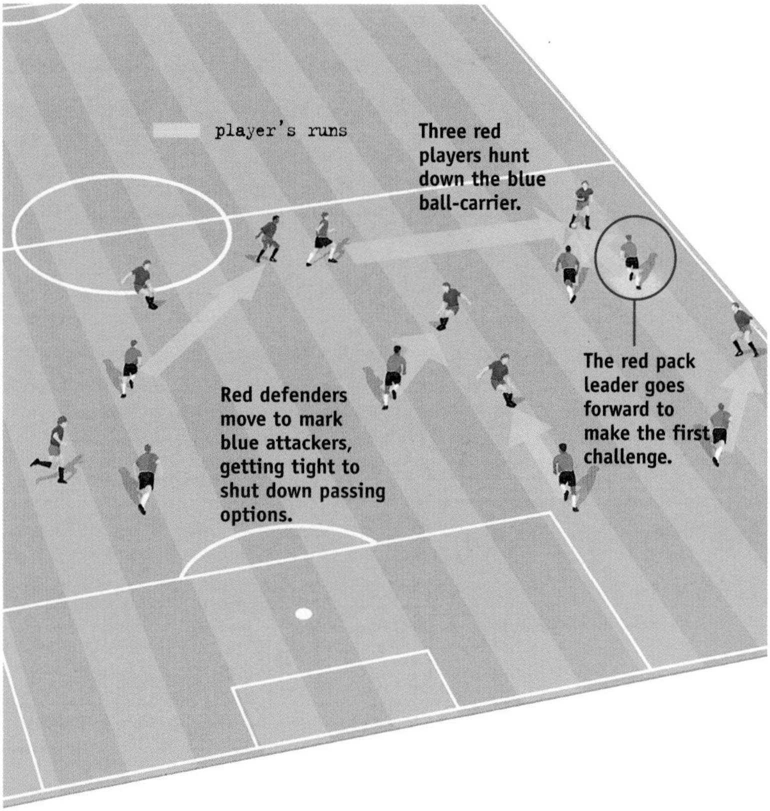

player's runs

Three red players hunt down the blue ball-carrier.

The red pack leader goes forward to make the first challenge.

Red defenders move to mark blue attackers, getting tight to shut down passing options.

Skills check

- Speed
- Awareness of team-mates
- Determination
- Quick decision-making
- Clear communication
- Tackling
- Anticipation
- Quick reactions
- Fitness

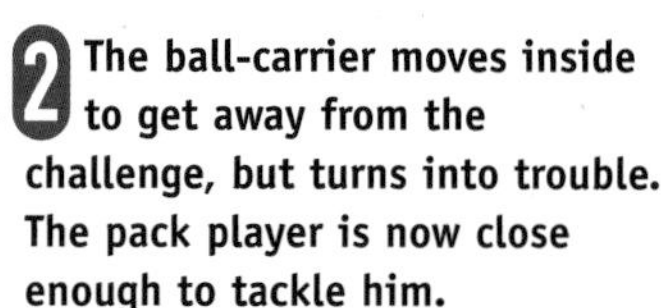

1 The red 'pack leader' comes in to make a challenge on the ball-carrier in blue. The supporting red player gets closer to cut off the passing or running options.

2 The ball-carrier moves inside to get away from the challenge, but turns into trouble. The pack player is now close enough to tackle him.

3 The pack player makes his challenge. The original pack leader continues to close in – to cover his team-mate and pick up the ball if it bounces loose.

Short passing

Good footballing sides always play a short passing game. It demands patience, great technique, constant movement off the ball and good communication, plus excellent ball control.

A good short pass is one that allows the receiver to control the ball effortlessly. This usually means playing to feet rather than into space, keeping the ball on the ground and making sure the pass is weighted correctly.

Making space

Short passing is not just about keeping possession of the ball for its own sake. The short pass is also very effective for creating space for other players to run into. If two or three players are playing keep-ball using short passes, defenders can lose patience and dive in to the tackle, leaving gaps in their defence which can then be exploited.

Coach says

- **Be quick, but don't lose the accuracy.**
- **Your body language can signal your intentions – don't make it obvious where and when you intend to pass.**
- **Don't pass if it gets a team-mate into trouble.**

Basics Pass and move

Practising passing and moving is the best way to learn the basics of linking up as a team.

For this drill, two groups of two players face each other in single file, 10m apart. The first person passes the ball to the player facing, then runs on to the back of the file opposite. The receiving player does the same in the other direction. Carry on until all players make five passes. Use both the inside and outside of each foot and concentrate on the weight, the timing and the accuracy of each pass.

Control the ball with just one touch, then pass it to the player opposite.

Make it accurate

This drill improves passing accuracy. Place two markers, 1m apart, betwee the groups. Now pass the ball throug the gap between the markers.

Practice drill

This drill for four players, played in a 10m square grid, is designed to develop your passing using the inside and outside of both feet. Repeat the drill then swap positions.

Four players stand at the centre of each side of the grid. The first player passes to the person opposite, who runs on to the ball and passes to the right with the outside of the foot. These two players swap positions. The receiving player passes to the player opposite – with the inside of either foot – who then passes to her left with the outside of the left foot.

Player A uses the inside of either foot to pass to B, who runs forward to meet the ball.

B takes one touch to control the ball and then passes to C using the outside of the right foot.

Players A and B then continue their runs to crossover and swap their positions on the grid.

C passes to D with the inside of the left or right foot. D runs forward and passes the ball to B with the outside of her left foot.

C and D now cross over. B then passes to A who starts the drill again. Repeat the exercise three times. Swap positions.

Use the side of the foot for straight passes.

Skills check

- ○ Good first touch and control
- ○ Skilful side-foot technique
- ○ Constant movement off the ball
- ○ Good communication

Playing to feet

The most efficient way of keeping the ball is to play it to feet. When a pass is played to any other part of the body, it often takes longer for the receiver to control – giving opponents more time to close in and win the ball. Passes should be easy for team-mates to control.

Skilful teams play to feet and move the ball forward accurately and at pace. This ensures that the receiver can control the ball quickly and so has time to use possession more effectively.

Think on your feet

Good vision and thinking ahead are vital if the tactic of playing to feet is to work to best effect. The passer must look for the runs of his team-mates and, by reading the game well, play the most useful ball.

Coach says

- **For greater accuracy, try to use the inside of the foot to play the ball to feet.**
- **Remember, one bad pass usually leads to another.**
- **Stay on your toes when you make yourself available for a pass. Then you can react quicker if the pass isn't perfect.**

Basics Be ready to receive

What every receiver wants is a pass that reaches him at a reasonable pace and slightly towards his stronger side. This will make controlling the pass easy. The ball ought to reach the receiver, although he should be ready to move forward if the pass is underhit.

Practise receiving the ball from a team-mate with a defender behind you putting pressure on. Stay on your toes so that you can react quickly to the pass.

1 Get on your toes before the ball is played to you – then you can react more quickly to the ball.

2 Control the ball and protect it by keeping your body between the ball and the defender.

3 Hit the return pass back to the feet of your team-mate firmly and accurately.

Practice drill

In this pass-and-move drill, one player starts in each corner of a 40 x 40m square. The players then follow these steps: (1) Player A plays the ball to B and follows his pass. (2) B returns the ball to A. (3) A then lays an angled ball back, to the left of B. (4) B passes the ball on to C and the drill continues in similar fashion on all sides of the square.

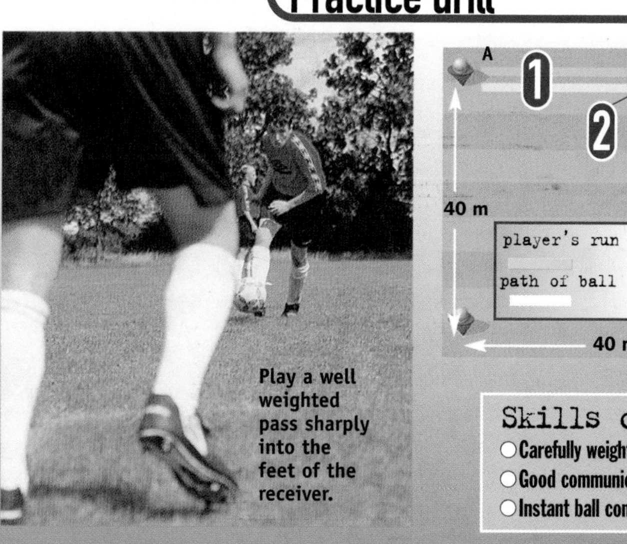

Play a well weighted pass sharply into the feet of the receiver.

Skills check

- Carefully weighted passes
- Good communication
- Instant ball control

Advanced Pass with pace

Playing to feet can lead to goals. To do so, the passing must be sharp and the lay-offs accurate and well weighted. Practise this tactical drill on a full-size pitch with one metal man (or cone) on the edge of the box and another 20 yards farther back. Each metal man has a player standing in front of it. One player runs with the ball from the halfway line, playing the ball to the feet of each standing player and taking a return. When he gets the ball back the second time, he goes for goal.

1 **After the first passing exchange, approach the second player and get the ball into his feet at pace.**

2 **Tell him which side you want the ball laid off. If hit just right, it should fall...**

3 **...perfectly into your path so that you can hit a first-time shot at the keeper.**

Playing into space

To move the ball quickly upfield, it is often best to play the ball into space. If you see some room in front of a team-mate, use it. Don't pass directly to him, so he has to stop and control the ball. Let him take it in full flight. To perform this tactic well, you need players willing to make intelligent runs into space and passers capable of hitting the ball accurately into the right area. The pass should be at such a pace that the receiver can run on to it without breaking stride.

Know your options

This tactic is particularly effective in attack. You can play balls down the wing for a player to run on to, or even better, hit the ball into the space behind the defence so a striker can run in on goal.

Coach says

- In order to play a ball into space effectively, players must weight their passes properly.
- Team-mates must be quick to spot where the ball is going.

Skills check

- Speed of thought
- Anticipation
- Vision
- Accurate delivery

Basics Knock it long

This drill, carried out on a 60 x 60m area divided into 20m strips (right), has one player in each team of four patrolling the strips at either end. When the ball is played to one of the lone players at the end, he has to flight it over the middle strip into one of the 10 x 20m corners using the correct weight and spin.

The lone clearing player has to loft the ball over the players in the middle and into the space at the far corners

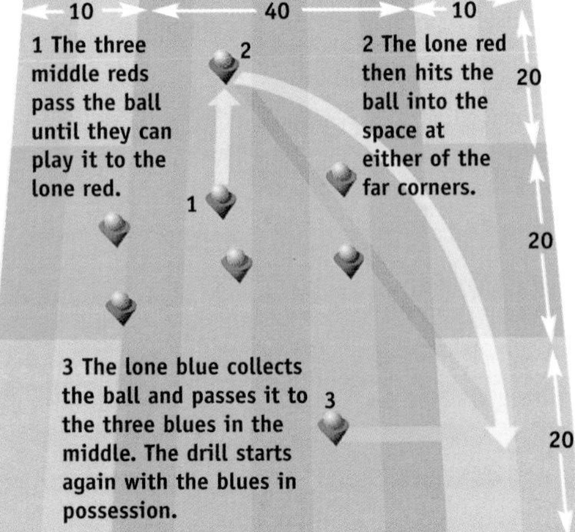

Practice drill

Using the basic drill, add a player to each team so eight players are in the central strip. When the ball is played to the lone player, he can play it into the whole 60 x 20m grid at the other end but two of the opposition can now enter his area to close him down.

The red clearing player gets his pass away before the blue player can close him down

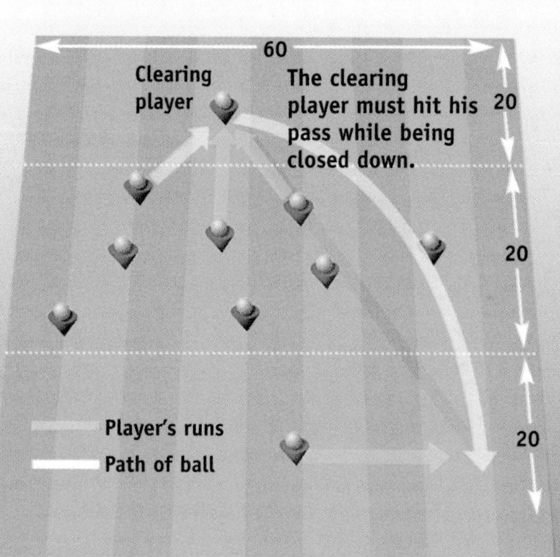

Advanced Make the decisive pass

Six red players take on five blue defenders and a keeper in a match-play situation. The defence push up – looking to catch the reds offside. A red player in possession must look for a team-mate's run and play the ball into space for him, making the defenders turn.

1 **Keep possession until one of your team-mates makes a run. Then play the ball into the space behind the defender.**

2 **Time the pass to avoid playing your team-mate offside and weight it so that he can take it in his stride as he runs.**

3 **Once the pass has been played, move to support your team-mate as he takes the ball forward to make a scoring opportunity.**

One-twos

Quick, one-touch football is always thrilling to watch. All top-class teams who play a passing game use the one-two, or wall pass.

The beauty of this move is that you can bypass a defender without the risky strategy of dribbling around him.

Outsmart the defence

Even the most organised and disciplined defence can be broken down by this clever interchange of passes. But remember, communication is essential when playing a one-two. If you see the possibility of a wall pass, call to the other player, 'One-two!' or 'Give it back!', and point to where you want the return ball to be played.

Coach says

- **Instead of trying to beat your opponent, lay the ball off and find space for a return pass.**
- **Communicate with your team-mates to set the move up.**
- **Get the return ball played into your path.**

Basics Pass, move and receive

Start by passing the ball across to a team-mate, then running on to receive the return (below).

Your team-mate should be about 7-8m in front of you at a 45° angle. The timing, weight and direction of the passes are all-important in this move in order to keep possession.

The first player passes directly to the second, who hits a first-time ball back into her path.

The first player passes to her team-mate and continues her run.

The second player lays the ball back into the path of the runner.

White arrow = direction of ball
Yellow arrow = direction of player

Take out the defender

To increase the difficulty of this exercise, include a defender (blue, above). The first orange attacker now has to off-load the ball under pressure. If the attacker leaves the pass too late, the defender will be able to get a challenge in. But if the attacker plays the ball too early, the defender will probably intercept the return pass.

Practice drill

Two groups – each containing orange attackers and blue defenders – stand 20m apart. (1) The first attacker runs with the ball from the top group. At the same time, a second attacker, together with a defender, run up from the bottom group. After running about 10m, the first attacker passes to the second. (2) The second attacker returns the pass to the first attacker around the defender. The defender's role is to add pressure and make sure the passes are played precisely. (3) The first attacker then passes the ball to the next attacker in the bottom group, who starts the whole move off again.

White arrow = direction of ball; Yellow arrow = direction of player

Advanced One-two your way to goal

Once you have perfected the one-two in practice drills, it is time to try it out on the pitch. You need three attackers, three defenders and a keeper.

The central attacker starts with the ball about 20m from goal. A defender puts her under pressure as she runs towards goal, looking to play a one-two either side of her. The other two attackers get ahead of their blue markers. Either can then receive a pass and set up the first attacker for a shot on goal.

The through-ball

The single most devastating pass in football is the perfectly played through-ball. It puts a striker clear of the defence, in metres of space, with only the keeper to beat.

The ideal pass is played between or over defenders and is delicately weighted for the attacker to run on to without breaking stride. It requires total understanding between striker and passer to get it right.

Into the gap

The striker must anticipate the through-ball and make a darting run towards the space behind the defence. The ball carrier must release his pass before the striker runs into an offside position. If both get it spot on, there is no way for the defence to respond in time.

Coach says

- Play it early. Don't delay your pass too long or the receiver will run offside.
- The receiver can reduce the risk of running offside by making diagonal runs.

Skills check

- Communication
- Awareness
- Timing
- Accurate passing
- Disguise

Basics Pass it through and beyond

This drill takes place in a 20 x 20m area, and helps develop the ability to manipulate defenders so that they are at your mercy for the through-ball.

Five red players try to keep possession, passing the ball around until they have succeeded in opening up a gap between the two blue players who are 'piggy in the middle'.

When they spot a gap, the red players must play an accurate through-ball between the defenders.

1 Player A draws the two blue defenders towards him. Player B signals to him that there's a gap and he can receive a pass.

2 Player A spots a safe opportunity for a through-ball and plays a side-footed pass to player B's left for him to run on to.

3 Player B starts to run on to the ball. Once he receives and controls the pass, the drill continues with the search for the next through-ball.

Practice drill

This is a seven-a-side match-play drill, played on a 60 x 40 pitch with two 10m-deep zones in front of the goals, occupied by the goalkeeper and one defender. The midfield players have to play through-balls into the 10m zones.

When a through-ball is played, an attacker is allowed to run into the 10m zone to receive the pass and attempt to set up a shot on goal. Other attackers and defenders can then follow. They can remain in the zone until a goal is scored, the ball is knocked out of play or the keeper gets hold of the ball.

Technique Use your feet

There are basically two types of through-ball: the longer pass around or over the defence and the shorter ball played between them.

For the longer through-ball, usually played from around the halfway line, you'll probably need to use your instep. If you are near your attackers, thread a side-foot pass through the defence.

USING THE INSTEP
If you are lofting the through-ball with the instep, try to put back-spin on the ball to stop it running through to the goalie. Strike the ball's underside and cut short the follow-through as in a chip.

USING THE SIDE OF THE FOOT
With the side of the foot, weight the through-ball so it is played directly into the striker's path.

Playing through each third

Although there are no actual thirds marked out on the pitch, coaches often refer to three playing zones: the defensive third, the midfield third and the attacking third. When teams build up a passing move through these zones rather than launching a long, high ball upfield, they are referred to as playing the ball through each third.

Back to front

To play this way, a team needs players who are comfortable in possession, skilled passers of the ball and good at running into space.

When the keeper gets the ball, he rolls it out to a defender rather than kicking it upfield. The defender's team-mates then offer themselves for short, simple passes and the team use these as the building blocks of the attack.

Coach says

- **Pass and move. That's the key to playing the ball through each third. Make sure your passes reach their target and then offer yourself for a pass later in the move.**
- **Opposing sides find it difficult to pick up defenders and midfielders who make attacking runs.**

Basics Pass and support

Practise playing the ball through each third of the playing area by dividing a 60 x 40m pitch into three 20 x 40m sections. A goalkeeper and defender play in the first third, two midfielders occupy the second third and a lone striker has to face an opposition goalkeeper in the final third.

To start the drill, the first keeper rolls the ball to the defender. By passing the ball accurately to their team-mates, the players move upfield to try to score.

Four outfield players pass the ball through each third of a 60 x 40m pitch and then attempt to score

1 The keeper rolls the ball to the defender, who looks to pass the ball forward.

2 The defender passes to a player in the middle third and runs on in support.

3 The midfielder passes to the attacker in the final third who shoots for goal.

Practice drill

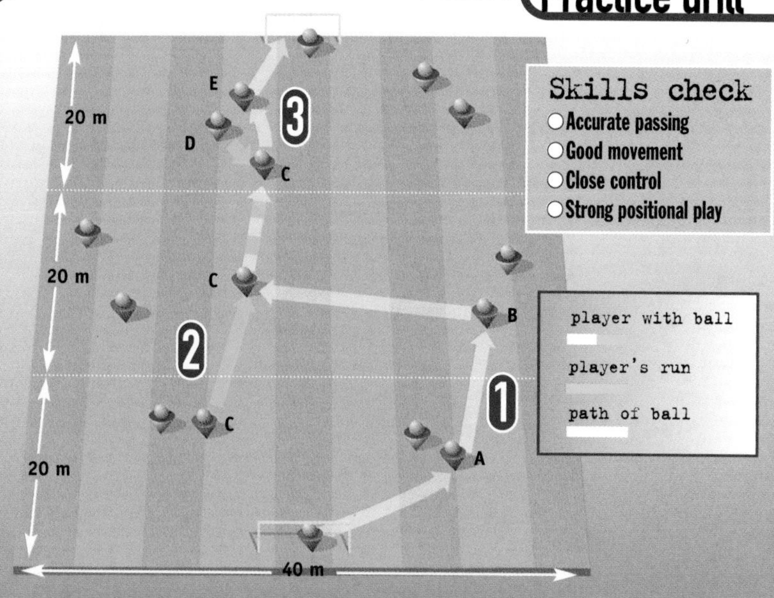

Skills check

- Accurate passing
- Good movement
- Close control
- Strong positional play

1 Red player A takes the ball from the keeper and passes on to player B.
2 Player C runs on to create an extra man in the middle zone.
3 Receiving the ball, C runs to the final third, draws the blue defender, D, and releases the free red player, E, to score.

Using the same pitch layout as in Basics, this drill is for two teams of six players plus two keepers. Two members of each team start in each third.

As each team launches an attack from one third to another, one attacking player is allowed to run into the next third, while his marker must stay behind. This creates a three against two situation in the middle and final thirds, and emphasises the value of teamwork through good support running.

Advanced Keep the ball moving forward

In this drill, take the tactic into open play with nine against nine (plus keepers) on a full-size pitch.

Try to play your way past the opposition by using accurate passing and good running off the ball. Make runs to create space for yourself or a team-mate, try clever one-twos, and always be on hand for a pass. Most importantly, keep possession and try to score.

1 Bringing the ball out of defence, the red player draws a blue player to him and passes.

2 The nearest red player begins a run to support the man on the ball and provide passing options.

3 Receiving the ball, he is through to the final third and prepares to cross.

Passing in the attacking third

In the attacking third of the pitch – where defenders minimise your time and space – it is essential that attackers can pass the ball under pressure. A series of simple, quick passes can open up gaps in the meanest defences.

Passport to goal

To pass your way through a defence, you need good vision and awareness to spot the runs of your team-mates and identify the best pass to play. You also have to be confident in playing the ball instantly with all parts of both feet – there will rarely be time to dwell on the ball.

Making the pass itself requires good judgement. You must hit the ball at the right time and speed to get your player in on goal at pace.

Coach says

- The key to attacking passing is looking up and assessing your options at speed.
- Instinctive control is vital – you can then look up for options rather than down at the ball.
- Make a good run after your pass – the one-two is a great way to get through a defence.

Basics Pass the ball through

Passing the ball in the attacking third, where time and space are so limited, requires concentration, vision and a confident touch.

When you get the ball in attack, you may only have a split-second to decide which pass to play. You should try to get used to taking a maximum of two touches on the ball – one to control it and another to pass. Quick passing enables you to pull defences apart and put your team through on goal.

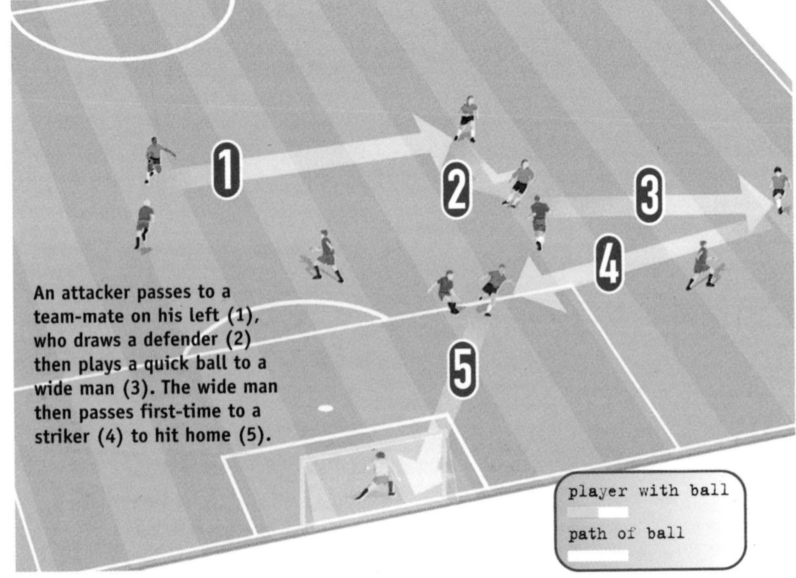

An attacker passes to a team-mate on his left (1), who draws a defender (2) then plays a quick ball to a wide man (3). The wide man then passes first-time to a striker (4) to hit home (5).

Practice drill

In this drill, a central player, A, acts as the passing link between three other players on the sides of a 15 x 20m zone.

A side player starts by passing to the middle man, who passes to one of the other two receivers. The new receiver must pass back to the middle man. Try to speed up your passing without losing accuracy.

15

The side players can move to the spare edge of the zone (above) during the drill.

A

20

Players may take a touch before passing.

All passes go through the middle man (A). He should not have too much time on the ball and must make a quick decision as to who to pass to next.

1 The middle man (A) controls the ball with one touch and is ready to pass it out again.

2 He adjusts his body position to pass the ball with the side of his foot out to the right.

Advanced Make six passes and shoot

This drill provides good practice for attacking with quick passing moves.

Two teams of three players attack two small goals on a 15 x 20m pitch. Before either team can shoot, they must first put together a move of six passes or more.

Good passing and movement are the key to winning the game.

You must complete six passes in a row before you have a shot at goal.

The player on the ball must stay in control and pick the best pass.

The receivers must find space and give their team-mate passing options.

Skills check
- Excellent awareness
- Good touch on the ball
- Coolness under pressure
- Speed of thought

Crossing from the byline

Good crosses make goals. They land, ideally, in front of the attacker just as he arrives to apply the finishing touch. The most dangerous place to deliver such a cross from is the byline.

When the ball is cut back from the byline, defenders will be facing towards their own goal. They are likely to be pressurised into knocking the ball out for a corner. At worst, they risk putting it into their own net and conceding an own goal.

Decision-making

To make the cross count, the player who gets to the byline must look up, decide where he is going to put his cross and deliver it accurately. If the cross is hit well, the attackers should be favourites to score.

Coach says

- When you get to the byline always look up and assess your options. Don't waste your position.
- Take all the time you've got to make sure your cross finds its target.
- Always hit your cross around or over the nearest defender. It should not be put too close to the goalkeeper.

Basics Push the pass

The golden rule for crossing from the byline is not to put the ball too close to the goalkeeper. Anything in the heart of the six-yard box – the red zone – becomes a virtual back pass and a waste of a good position. If you see an attacker unmarked in one of the danger zones below, hit the ball to him.

Try to play the ball either to the striker's head or to his feet so that he can take a first-time shot.

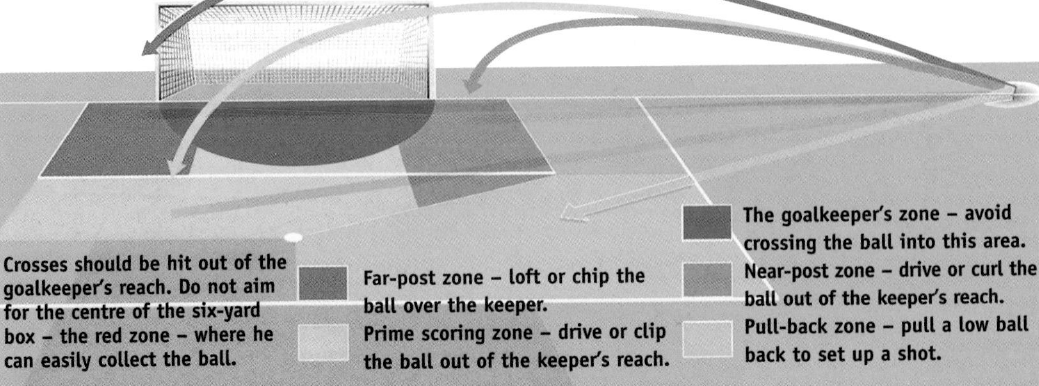

Technique Curl the ball away from goal

The best way to make sure the ball stays out of reach of the goalkeeper is to curl it away from him – and the byline is the best place from which to do this.

A curling cross moves back into the path of the strikers who are coming in. It may also lure the keeper out of position as he tries to claim the cross.

Skills check

- Pace
- Awareness
- Good crossing technique

1 As you hit the ball, lean away in the direction you want it to curl.

2 Hit through the side of the ball to get spin to make it swerve.

3 If you want to loft your cross, lean back and follow through.

Advanced Miss out the first defender

This drill should be run at game pace on a half pitch with the emphasis on quality of delivery. From outside the penalty area, an attacker plays the ball into the path of a winger and then runs towards goal. At the same time, a defender sets off from the edge of the penalty area to close down the winger. The winger must get to the byline and put in a cross, so the attacker has a chance to score.

1 The ball is played into the path of the running winger.

2 He looks up to assess his options as he takes the ball to the byline.

3 He outruns his marker to create enough space to put in a cross.

4 As he reaches the byline, he crosses into the danger zone.

Switching play

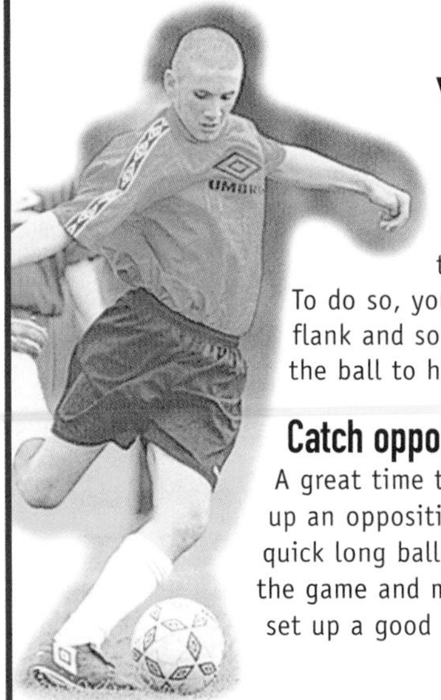

Your team is attacking down one of the wings but several opposition players are blocking your progress and stopping you going forward.

A good solution is to switch play across the pitch where there are fewer defenders. To do so, you need a player to make a run on the other flank and someone with the vision and ability to play the ball to him and thus strand many of the opposition.

Catch opponents out

A great time to switch play is when you have just broken up an opposition attack down the wing. By playing a quick long ball to the other wing, you change the focus of the game and may catch the opposition undermanned to set up a good attack for your team.

Coach says

- If you're part of an attack down one wing, keep your head up and look around. There may be an easier way forward on the other wing.
- Whenever possible, send your switch pass behind the defence, especially if you're passing to a quick winger.

Skills check

- Accurate passers of the ball on both sides of pitch
- Speed of thought
- Speed of execution – fast players to run into available space

Basics Make it happen fast

The ideal switch pass is played quickly behind the defence – a slow ball is likely to be intercepted and picked up by the defenders. You should not just 'hit and hope' – make sure there is a team-mate to run on to the pass.

The switch pass is often most effective when played into the space in front of a fast-running wing back or winger. He can take the ball down the wing and then put a telling cross into the penalty area for your forwards to attack.

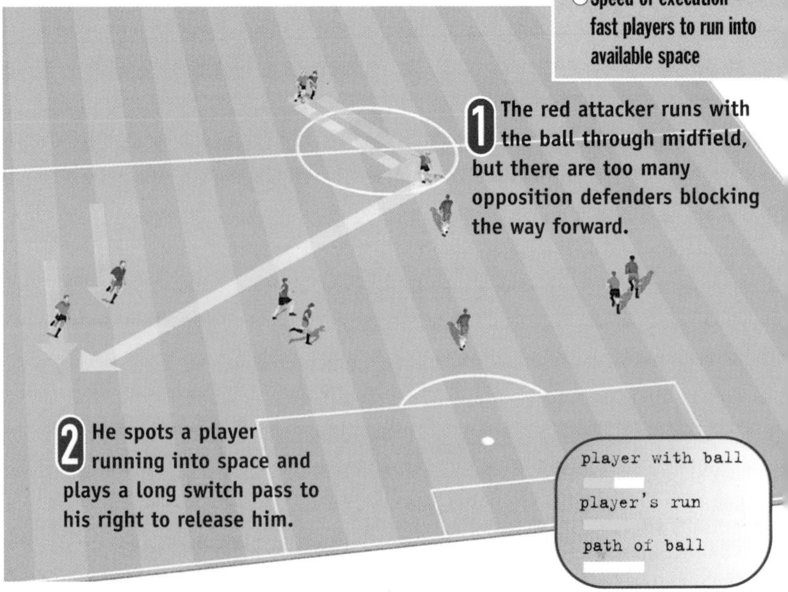

1 The red attacker runs with the ball through midfield, but there are too many opposition defenders blocking the way forward.

2 He spots a player running into space and plays a long switch pass to his right to release him.

Practice drill

To switch play, you need to hit accurate long passes. In this drill, players pass the ball to and from the corners of a 40 x 40m square. The first player passes to a player at any of the other corners, then runs to that corner. The receiver then passes to another corner to continue the drill.

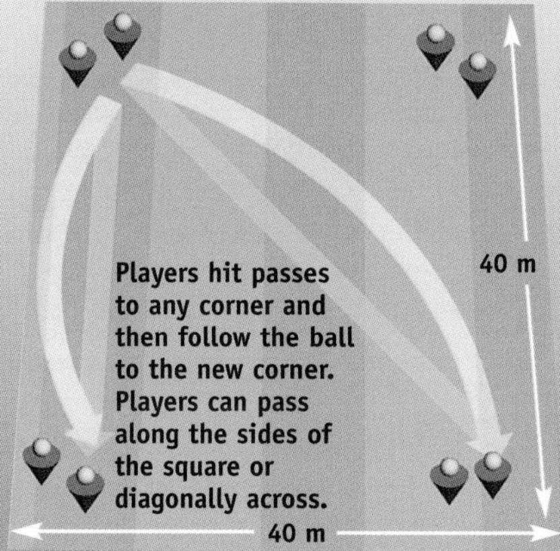

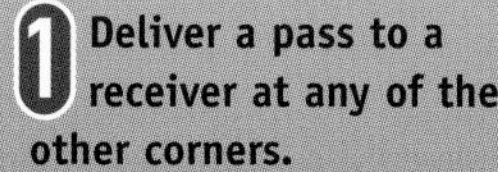

1 Deliver a pass to a receiver at any of the other corners.

2 After your pass, run to the same corner. The faster the drill, the better.

Advanced Bring the trick into play

Fine-tune your switching play skills with this match-play drill. Six attackers try to score against six defenders and a goalkeeper on a half-sized pitch.

The aim is to build a controlled attack, drawing markers out of position to create an opportunity for the switch. When you have found space, exploit it quickly, before the defence shuts you down.

1 The two red players are building an attack down the flank. One passes to the other as the defence closes in.

2 The player who receives the ball is now hemmed in by defenders and cannot pass back to his team-mate without losing possession.

3 A switch pass away from the defenders to a red player on the other wing keeps the attack going and strands the defence.

Possession play

To master the art of possession, football teams need to develop both control skills and tactical play. By constantly passing it to each other they can pull opposing defenders out of position, frustrate them into making rash tackles and create the space for a penetrating pass which will find a route to goal.

Teams who retain possession by playing keep-ball dominate the action. This also demoralises the opposition into making mistakes – leaving gaps which create opportunities to score.

Confidence and ability

The ability to keep possession does not mean that you will always win a match, but good passing sides can turn possession into goals. After all, you can only score when you have the ball.

Coach says

- Look to play the ball behind the defence.
- Find space off the ball to create more passing options for your team.
- Possession play should have an end product – a final, penetrating pass leading to a shot on goal.

Basics Build slowly from the back

Passing sides often build from the back. Instead of kicking the ball upfield, the keeper will roll or kick it to a defender. But the ball will only be played forward when possession can be retained – so players have to stay constantly on the move.

In the example on the right, the yellow arrows show the players' runs – while the orange shading shows the areas in which they are likely to receive the ball.

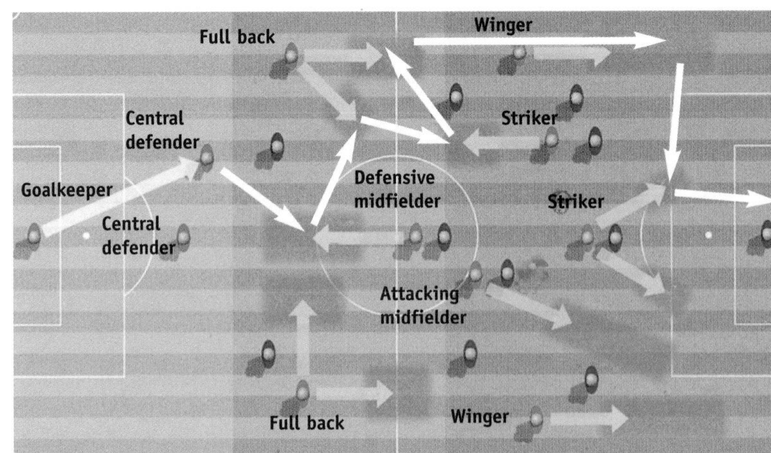

The red team plays a passing game, building an attack slowly into the first shaded zone then the second. The white arrows suggest one route to goal.

White arrow = direction of ball
Yellow arrow = direction of player

Practice drill

For this three-man drill, two orange attackers attempt to retain possession despite the attentions of a blue defender in a 10 x 10m grid.

Movement off the ball is vital to ensure that the defender does not intercept or make a successful tackle. A sure and confident touch on the ball will also help to evade and frustrate the defender as he tries to win possession.

1 As the blue defender closes in, the orange player looks for support from his team-mate.

2 He lays the ball off, bypassing the defender with a well-weighted, measured pass.

3 Then he moves to lend support, creating a better angle ready for the return pass.

Advanced Make your passing positive

The hallmark of a top passing side is the ability to keep possession in the final third of the pitch, where space and time are limited. This exercise calls for a good first touch, movement off the ball and crisp passing.

This drill, played on a 10 x 10m grid, is for four orange attackers and two defenders in blue. Attackers score a 'goal' each time they string together five consecutive passes, or play a pass which splits the defence. When the attackers are dispossessed three times, teams are changed so everyone plays as an attacker and a defender.

Skills check

- Good ball control
- Mastery of passing techniques
- Confidence to switch the play from flank to flank

Players need to make precise passes to team-mates in space

Attackers need confidence to split the defence if the chance arises

Holding up the ball

Every team needs a player who can keep possession when the ball is played upfield. Whether you are a striker or a midfielder, you must be able to hold on to the ball so that supporting players can join the attack. If you fail, the ball will soon be heading back to your goal.

Shield the ball

A player skilled at this art – often called 'an outlet' – is a terrific asset to his team. He can turn and take on his marker or lay the ball off and bring his team-mates into the game.

Top players have great ability to shield the ball, using superb touch to control it instantly and their body strength to fend off defenders.

Coach says

- **Make yourself available when your team clears from defence.**
- **Position your body side-on to keep the opposition away from the ball.**
- **Once you have held up the ball, be aware of the supporting runs of your team-mates.**

Basics Stay strong

In this basic exercise, the ball is played to an attacker by a feeder. The attacker is marked from behind by a defender. He has to hold the ball, using his body to shield it from the defender, and then lay it back to the feeder with an accurate pass.

Get your body between the ball and the defender and be sure you stand firm so that he cannot push you off the ball.

1 Before the attacker receives the ball, he uses his arm to keep the defender at bay.

2 When he gets the ball, he keeps his arms out for balance and leans into the defender.

3 After he has the ball under control, he plays a simple side-foot pass back to the feeder.

Advanced Get your body side-on

Now do the same drill with a team-mate on either side of you. You now have three passing options: left, right or back to the feeder.

Try to get side-on when you receive the ball, so it is farther from the defender. This also expands your options – you can more easily play the ball to the side.

1 The attacker takes the ball on the outside of the foot, creating a long barrier.

2 The defender is so far from the ball, his only hope of winning it is to lunge across the striker.

3 Having controlled the ball, the attacker now plays a side-foot pass to the team-mate on his left.

Skills check

- Close control
- Strength on the ball
- Awareness of team-mates
- Good turning ability
- Weighted passing

Practice drill

This drill uses two defenders and two attackers in a 20 x 10m grid. One attacker plays the ball from one of the 10m lines to the other attacker. The second attacker must hold the ball up, and then lay the ball back to the first attacker who has made a supporting forward run.

The attackers then have to link up so they eventually run the ball over the opposite 10m line.

1 With a defender behind him attacker A receives the pass and holds up the ball.

2 When attacker B gets in a position to support, attacker A lays the ball back and spins off his marker.

3 B can now play a through-ball to A and give him the chance to get the ball to the end of the grid.

Support play

Good support play is essential to most attacking moves. When one of your players is on the ball, he should have team-mates getting into space around him, taking up positions that will make a potential pass easy to play.

The greater the number of options you create, the less predictable your team becomes.

Look, listen and lay it off

Remember, playing backwards to keep possession is better than a ball forward which may be intercepted.

Players supporting a move should tell the man on the ball where they are. He must listen for these calls and keep his head up to view his options – if the supporting players have pulled defenders away, he can choose to continue the attack himself.

Coach says

- **Support play doesn't mean getting as close as possible to the man on the ball. It means finding space in as good a position as possible anywhere around him.**
- **Use support play to keep the ball moving. As soon as it stops, defenders will be able to regroup.**

Basics Seek out space

Supporting the man on the ball means giving him an angle – getting into a position where the line of a potential pass is not blocked by a defender.

This requires intelligent running off the ball by the players in support. They need to get into space within range of the man in possession and must try to lose their markers. If the supporting player is at risk of being tackled as soon as he gets the ball, he is not a helpful option for a pass.

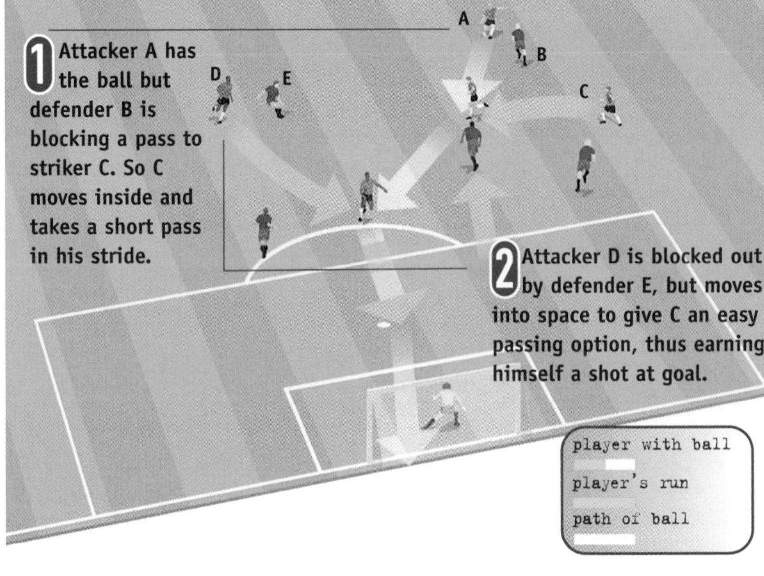

Practice drill

In this drill, four play four on a 20 x 20m grid, with the object being to string as many passes together as possible.

Help comes in the form of two neutral players patrolling the boundaries of the grid, who can join in with the side that has the ball.

By using these extra supporting players and making runs themselves, the team in possession can help the man on the ball and control the game.

Skills check
- Intelligent movement
- Good communication
- Slick passing
- Excellent vision

Two red defenders close down the blue player on the ball. But one of his team-mates begins a supporting run and calls for the ball. The player in possession also has the option of using the player behind him.

Advanced Develop 360° support

Five play five in a 30 x 30m square in this advanced drill. Dotted around inside the grid are four 1m-wide mini goals. In order to score, a player must pass the ball to a team-mate through a goal. The drill is intended to make the man on the ball look all around him for the easiest pass to play. The supporting players must create options for him in all directions.

1 Red player A calls for the ball and makes a run into space, while his team move to support.

2 Red player B gets into position behind a gate to create a scoring opportunity.

3 Intelligent positioning and support play mean a goal is scored for the red team.

Counter-attack

This match-winning tactic involves turning defensive play into attack with a lightning-quick break. It can be a devastating manoeuvre, since it catches the opposition upfield and out of position. But to be effective the ball needs to be transferred very quickly from one end of the pitch to the other – and this means that the players involved must be superbly fit and fast, as well as accurate.

Ready with support

A counter-attack should be launched as soon as the opponents' attack breaks down. It is vital that each player involved knows exactly what the others are doing and can be ready quickly to offer support. Swift, incisive counter-attacks will unsettle any opposition and can also result in exciting goals.

Coach says

- Look for the long ball first. Make sure it is accurate.
- Forward support players should make diagonal runs.
- Attack any space in front of you if you have the ball.
- Support quickly.

Basics Attack as a team

The aim of a counter-attack is simple: as soon as your team win the ball all players should think of attacking and start to go forward as a unit.

Front players should move into good receiving positions, while midfield players need to get forward in support. Each player must produce penetrating and accurate passes. An example of how this can work is shown right.

White arrow = direction of ball
Yellow arrow = direction of player

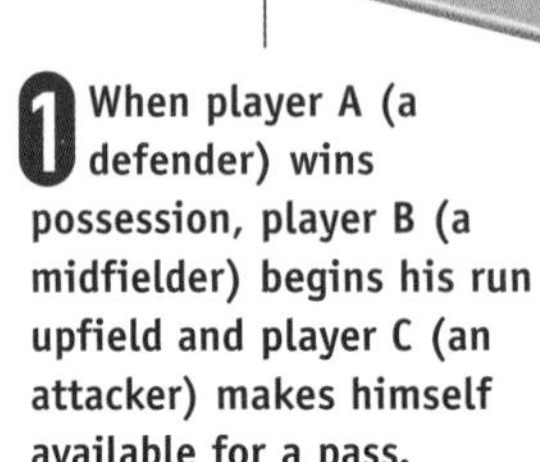

1 When player A (a defender) wins possession, player B (a midfielder) begins his run upfield and player C (an attacker) makes himself available for a pass.

2 Player C receives player A's long pass and makes a short run to the halfway line. Player B continues his run upfield at speed.

3 A short pass from player C sets player B in on goal. He takes the ball to the edge of the box before firing it past the keeper.

Practice drill

Player A, having made his pass, sets off in support

The receiving player B passes to C and runs to his spot

To encourage players to break quickly when the ball is played forward, practice this simple pass-and-move drill in a 10 x 10m square with six players and one ball.

Player A passes to any of his team-mates – in this case player B. As he passes the ball, A runs across the grid following the ball and takes B's place on the edge of the square.

Meanwhile, B passes to another player, in this case player C, and follows the ball to offer support. Decide where your pass is going to go before you receive the ball to help you work accurately and quickly. This drill relies on speed to be effective.

Make it more difficult with one-touch passing, calling out to the player you are passing to.

Skills check
- Good understanding
- Willingness to give immediate support in attack
- Peak fitness
- Lightning pace

Advanced Make the break

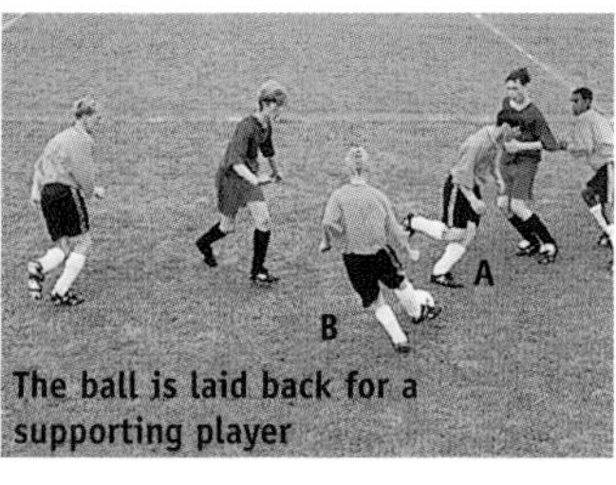

The ball is laid back for a supporting player

...who passes to the overlapping player

...who moves the play upfield using support

Six orange attackers and four blue defenders play on three 10m squares set in a row. Four attackers and two defenders start at one of the end squares.

Two attackers break free to run upfield. They take the ball across the middle square (no-man's land) and into the square at the other end (shown above), where they join two other support players in orange.

The aim is to pass the ball quickly to a team-mate, so that he can turn the play around and move back upfield to the first square. One of the attackers (A) passes to the support player B, who passes to the overlapping player C, who returns to the first square with D in support.

Creating space off the ball

An essential element of attacking play is movement off the ball. Look at all the great strikers and you will notice how they are making darting runs into space the moment their team gains possession.

Draw the defender

If a defender picks up a striker who is on a run, it will create space for the player in possession. If the defender does not pick up the striker, he will be available for a pass from the player on the ball.

Movement off the ball is very important whenever a player approaches goal with the ball. He needs his team-mates to draw defenders away from central positions so he can bring the ball up and score.

Coach says

- Time your run and call for the ball so that defenders will cover your movement.
- Keep on the move. Any movement will create trouble for defenders.
- When close to the last line of defence, make sure you do not run offside.

Basics Keep on the move

For this drill, two attackers take on one defender within a 20 x 10m grid. One attacker in orange (A) has to lure the defender in blue away with an off-the-ball run, while attacker B runs the ball up from the 20m line. A's run creates space for B to run up to the 10m line with the ball.

1 Attacker A makes a run across the grid and pulls her marker with her. This creates space for player B to exploit.

2 With the defender in blue concentrating on attacker A's movement, attacker B can run unchecked with the ball.

3 Attacker B makes it to the 10m line before the defender, realising her error, can get back to cover her.

Practice drill

In this pitch drill, three attackers in orange take on three defenders. Two of the attackers drag their markers wide, creating space for the attacker with the ball to shoot.

Skills check

- Good awareness
- Speed off the mark
- Good understanding with your team-mates

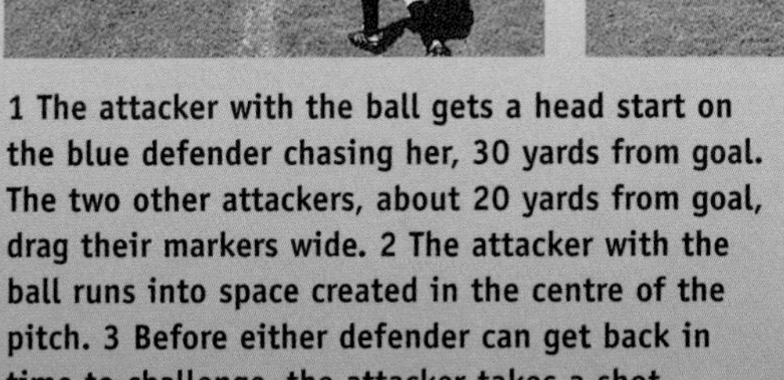

1 The attacker with the ball gets a head start on the blue defender chasing her, 30 yards from goal. The two other attackers, about 20 yards from goal, drag their markers wide. 2 The attacker with the ball runs into space created in the centre of the pitch. 3 Before either defender can get back in time to challenge, the attacker takes a shot.

Advanced Look for the return ball

Two attackers in orange take on three blue defenders in this pitch drill. To help create space, the attacker who starts with the ball (A) can pass as well as shoot.

The move shown below is usually referred to as an overlap. Attacker A plays a one-two with her fellow attacker (B), opening up space on the right flank and creating a shooting opportunity.

Note the way that attacker B runs in on goal as A is taking her shot. That way, if the ball rebounds off the post or the keeper, B is ready to pounce on the ball and slot it home.

B

A

A

1 Attacking player A, about 25 yards out from goal, plays a short pass to team-mate B.

2 Attacker A then moves into space on the right flank, ready to receive the return ball.

3 Attacker A collects the pass. She now has the space to run to goal or, as here, take the keeper by surprise with a long-range shot.

The overlap

A well-executed overlap is dangerous and difficult to stop. It puts an attacking player in space on the wing and, unless the marking is very sharp, behind the defence.

Make that run

The overlapping player simply overtakes the player in possession on the outside. If his run is spotted and a defender goes with him, he has at least managed to draw that defender out of position and created space for other players.

If not, a pass into his path sends him speeding down the wing. From there, any cross is difficult for defenders to deal with. They're running back and facing their own goal while attackers stream in to apply the finishing touch.

Coach says

- **Be equally prepared to receive the ball or to act as a decoy.**
- **Try to disguise the start of your run. By the time the defender has realised what you're doing, you should already be running into space.**

Basics Time it right

The key to the overlap is timing. The overlapping player (B) must learn to time and angle his run so that he receives the ball in full flight. The passer (A) must make sure he times his pass so that the overlapping player can run on to it without breaking stride. And together, the two attackers must communicate with each other. If the pass and the timing of the run are co-ordinated, the defender (C) is unable to intercept or tackle and is completely taken out of the game.

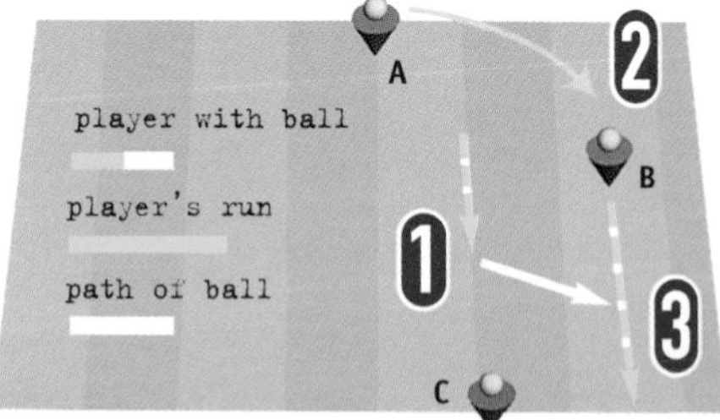

1 **As attacker A runs with the ball he draws defender C towards him. The second attacker (B) then begins his overlapping run from behind the first attacker.**

2 **The overlapping attacker arches his run so that he has space to receive the pass. If he runs too close to his fellow attacker, the defender may be able to intercept the pass.**

3 **The ball is played in front of the overlapping attacker. The pass is weighted so that he can run on to the ball without breaking stride and continue to attack at speed.**

Practice drill

This is a six-a-side match-play drill, played on a 60 x 40m pitch with a 5m-wide zone marked out along both wings. The 5m zone is there for overlapping runs. Only the team in possession can enter this zone, so any attacker making an overlap will be unchallenged.

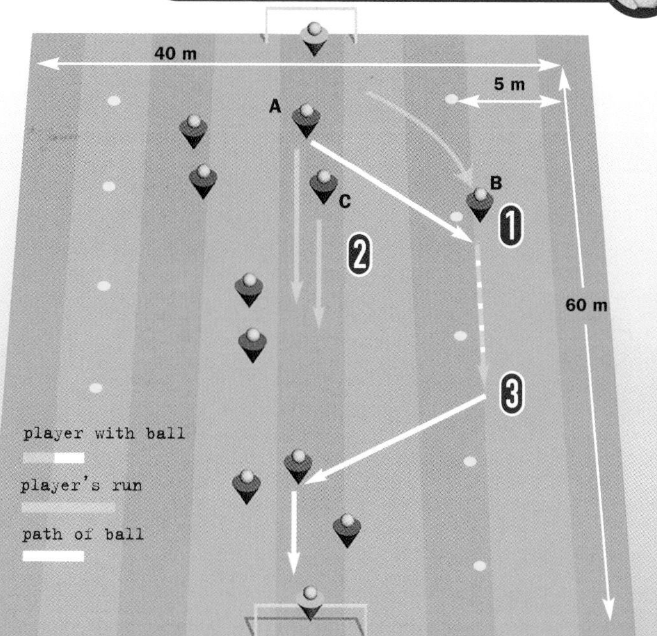

Skills check

- Awareness
- Understanding
- Timing
- Communication
- Short passing
- Explosive pace

1 The overlapping player B makes a run into the 5m zone and receives the ball from his team-mate A.

2 The blue defender C is completely taken out of the game. He has failed to tackle attacker A or intercept his pass and now has to back-track towards goal.

3 Before the defender can get back into a good defensive position, the overlapping attacker plays a dangerous cross into the area. (Note the way player A has followed up the attack after playing the initial pass.)

Using width in attack

Watch how any good team on the attack will get men out wide. Even if they don't have out-and-out wingers, they'll have wing-backs or wide midfielders running wide looking for the ball.

Wing it

With support down the wings, a central midfielder carrying the ball forward has many options. If defenders have been drawn out to mark the players on the wing, he can exploit gaps in the middle. If the defenders stay in the centre, he can pass out wide to instigate an attack on the wing.

Whichever option he chooses, he is stretching the defenders out of their formation, making them work hard and creating attacking opportunities.

Coach says

- **Get players wide as quickly and as often as you can. This will achieve your primary aim of stretching the defence.**
- **When a team-mate has the ball out wide, make an overlapping run to lure his marker away and leave more gaps in the defence.**

Basics Get players on the wing

Using width in attack can work in two ways. If you get the bailout wide, defenders must move out to win it back. Your wide man can then cross the ball into the space left in the middle.

The second way is shown on the right. If your players make runs out wide, the defenders are drawn out wide to mark them. This leaves spaces in the middle for your other attackers to exploit.

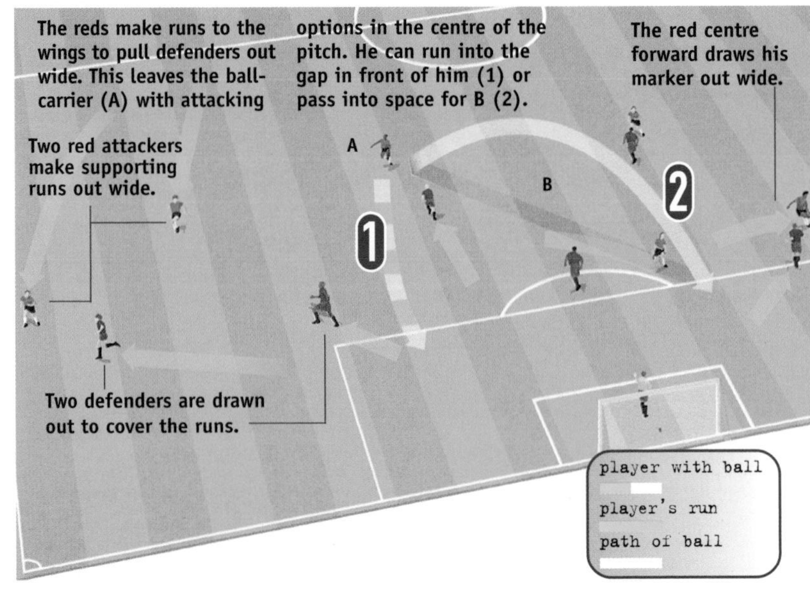

Practice drill

In a six versus six game on a 60 x 40m pitch, a 10 x 10m 'crossing zone' is created in each corner. The teams must get the ball into a crossing zone before they can go for goal. By passing and running in support, the players get width in their attacks, stretch the defence and score.

1 A red player makes an overlapping run into the crossing zone.

2 A blue defender is drawn out wide, creating more space in the middle.

3 From the wing, the red player is able to whip a dangerous cross into the penalty area.

Advanced Go wide to get ahead

Getting the ball wide not only stretches the defence, but also gives you a great spot from which to cross the ball.

Set up a six versus six game on a half pitch, with a 10 yard-wide zone on each wing occupied only by a wide man. The two wide men link up with whichever team is going forward – using the wide men well gives the attacking side the edge.

Skills check

- Communication
- Good support play
- Vision
- Sound passing ability

You can only get an advantage in this drill by using the wide men (in white shirts). Here the defenders struggle to close down the wide man and are in trouble when he crosses (inset).

Diagonal runs in attack

The modern forward is fit, fast and ever alert. He has to be. During every game he makes countless runs but gets the ball only a small percentage of the time.

Diagonal runs are one of the cleverest ploys in the game. The striker moves across the pitch in front of the defence to stay onside, dragging his marker with him. Then, with perfect timing, he darts forward diagonally. As the ball is played into space, he meets it with a speedy run.

Know your angles

The striker's run gives the passer a good angle to play a simple ball, but it makes life difficult for the defender, who has to keep up with the striker as he changes direction and pace to find an opening.

Coach says

- When you make a diagonal run, your first priority is to stay onside. This means not running beyond the last defender before the ball is played to you.
- Make sure your runs are sharp and explosive. Use speed to leave the defender behind.

Basics Time your run with the passer

The success of any diagonal run in attack depends on the timing of both the runner and the passer, both of which must be impeccable in order to beat the offside trap.

In the illustration (right), the midfielder must pass before the striker crosses in front of the last defender and strays offside. A good midfielder will read the striker's run and play a perfectly weighted ball for him to run on to. The pass should be heavy enough to beat the defence, but not run on to be gathered by the keeper.

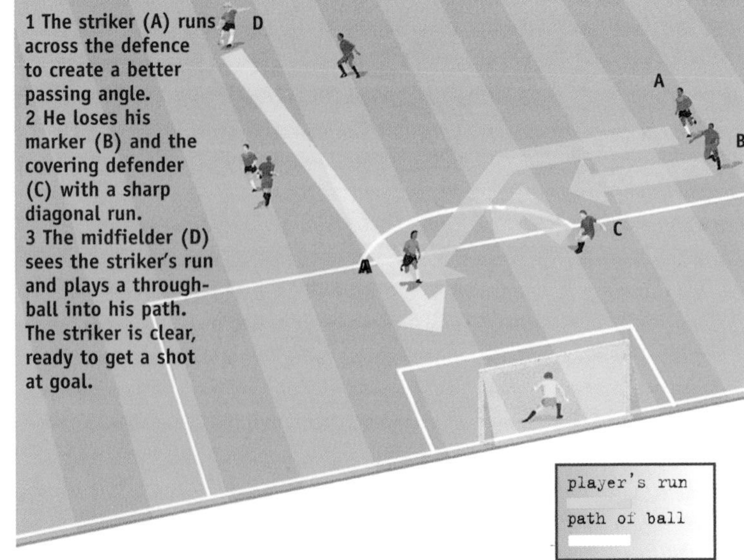

Practice drill

Good understanding between players is vital to make the diagonal run an effective attacking weapon. This drill works on the main principles of timing and passing.

Two players start their runs at the same time, 20m apart from each other. One runs with the ball and passes to the other – not to his feet but in such a way that he has to make a diagonal run to meet it.

Once you have got the timing right, try the drill with a goal and a keeper to perfect the weighting of the pass.

1 Player A starts with the ball and takes it forward. At the same time, player B runs forward.

2 After 5m or so, B makes his diagonal run and calls for the ball. A passes the ball to meet B's run.

Skills check
- Awareness
- Vision
- Patience
- Timing
- Speed off the mark

Advanced Beat the defenders

In this drill, players practise making diagonal runs in a match, set up on a 60 x 40m grid containing three 20 x 40m zones. Each side has six outfield players. Two players from each side operate in each zone and the two defensive duos at either end are encouraged to play offside.

The role of the attackers is to make diagonal runs off the ball and beat the offside trap. Even if they don't receive a pass themselves, the attackers will create space behind them which their team-mates will be able to exploit to keep the pressure on.

1 Make your diagonal run into space. Signal to the player in possession where you want the pass to be played.

2 Explode away from your marker – the element of surprise should give you an edge in the race to the ball.

3 Run on to the ball, assess your options and either cross the ball to a team-mate or, as here, take a first-time shot.

When to shoot

There is a saying in football – never pass when you can shoot. Knowing when to shoot requires split-second decision making, plus the confidence and ability to go for goal. You must have an appetite for scoring, and never be afraid to shoot as soon as you get a sight of goal.

Shoot quickly or pass

If you can see a clear path to goal, try a shot. If a team-mate is in a better position than you to score, lay the ball off instead. But whatever you decide, you must do it with lightning speed. A split-second's hesitation at the vital moment will probably mean the chance is lost.

Coach says

- Shoot if you get a chance – or even just half a chance.
- Pass if a team-mate is in a better position to score.
- Whenever you can see a direct line from the ball to the goal, take a shot.

Basics Work out your playing zone

Shots from a narrow angle are easier to save than shots from in front of goal. If you are out wide or close to the byline, your shooting angle will probably be quite narrow. In these situations it is usually a better idea to lay the ball back for one of your team-mates rather than shoot for goal.

Practice drill

For this exercise, a feeder passes the ball to an attacker, who shoots first time. Passes come from three positions:
(1) From behind: The feeder plays the ball through and the striker runs on to the pass and shoots first time, using either foot.
(2) From the side: The feeder plays the ball in from the right, then the left; the striker shoots first time with the foot nearest the ball, then with the foot furthest from it.
(3) From the front (shown below): The feeder lays the ball back to the striker, who shoots first time, keeping the ball low to make it harder for the goalkeeper to get down to make the save.

The feeder rolls the ball back to the striker, who shoots first time.

Receiving the lay-back, the striker keeps the ball down.

Skills check

- Quick decision-making
- Good first touch
- Ability to use both feet
- Accuracy
- Good timing
- Ability to remain calm and composed under pressure

Advanced Learn to shoot on sight

Set up a small-sided game on a pitch 30 x 20m. Get teams into four against four, with two more teams of four on the touchline ready to play.

Play two-touch football. You can either pass or shoot, but you are only allowed two touches or less – one touch to control the ball and one to pass or shoot. Goalkeepers distribute the ball.

Players will receive the ball within 25m of the goal so should be looking to shoot at the first opportunity.

The first team to score two goals wins and stays on to play a new team, for a maximum of three games.

The defender in blue has left the orange attacker with a clear sight of goal

The orange attacker shoots before the blue defender can get across to cover

One-on-one with the keeper

You've beaten the offside trap and the nearest defender is trailing 10 yards behind. As you near the penalty area, the goalkeeper charges off his line to narrow the angle. All of a sudden, being one-on-one with the keeper is not as easy as it looks.

Assess your options – whatever you choose, stick to it and remain calm.

Skills check

- Cool, calm approach
- Good balance
- Close control
- Confidence
- Accurate shot

Basics Watch the keeper

player with ball | player's run | path of ball

Good strikers first assess the keeper's positioning before deciding how they are going to try to score.

All keepers come off their lines to meet the threat, but it's a question of how far and how fast. Three possible positions for the keeper are shown here, along with the attacker's best chance of scoring in each case.

SHOOT EARLY
If the keeper stays back, shoot early – you'll have a large target area to aim at.

CHIP THE KEEPER
If the keeper advances halfway, you can chip the ball over him.

ROUND THE KEEPER
If the keeper closes you down quickly, try to take the ball round him.

Timed pactice

The aim of this drill is to beat the keeper at speed. Adapted from the American method of settling drawn games, it is known as a shoot-out. The striker begins his run to goal from the edge of the centre circle. He then has seven seconds to score.

Keep the ball under control and watch the keeper before deciding on the best route to goal, but remember that time is running out.

1 The striker advances and bides his time...

2 ...until the keeper moves. He then jinks left...

3 ...leaving the keeper stranded and the goal open.

Rounding the keeper

The sight of an attacker clean through on goal and facing a one-on-one with the keeper means a goal, or a brave save, is in the offing. For players, glory or disappointment awaits. Rounding the keeper and 'passing' the ball into an unguarded net is every striker's dream, but the manoeuvre takes confidence, skill and quick-thinking.

Skills check
- Confidence and composure on the ball
- Ability to change pace
- Good close control
- Flair for feinting

Basics Beat the last line of defence

To round the keeper successfully, you must practise approaching the goal and trying to disguise which side you will take the ball. Keep the ball close to your feet, as a brave goalkeeper will be able to pounce and steal possession if you give her the slightest chance.

1 Decide which way to round the keeper. Try to get her off balance, or, better still, get her to dive by feinting to shoot.

2 You must now change direction suddenly and accelerate past the keeper – making sure you keep the ball out of her reach.

3 Once past her, make sure you hit the target. You have beaten everyone, so take a moment to steady yourself before shooting.

Practice drill

Decide which way to round the keeper... **...take the ball past her without losing control...** **...then pass the ball on to one of your team-mates.**

Five players form a circle round a 10m grid and pass the ball to each other. The keeper stands in the middle of the circle, turning so that she is always facing the ball. When the coach gives the call, the player with the ball dribbles around the goalkeeper. Having rounded the keeper, the ball is passed to the next player. She in turn rounds the keeper and passes it to someone else.

It is important that players move back to the grid boundary each time to give the attacking player enough room in which to round the keeper.

Throw-ins

With a little invention, throw-ins can be more than just a means of getting the ball back into play. A well executed throw-in routine in your opponent's half can become a valuable attacking ploy. So the throw-in should be treated as a set piece – rehearse different variations on the training ground.

Attacking weapon

Getting the most out of a throw-in requires good basic throwing technique and sharp, intelligent movement from potential receivers. In this way, a throw-in can be used to create space for your team and spark an attack.

Coach says

- Take throw-ins properly. Throw the ball forward, not down.
- Make 'decoy' throws (without releasing the ball) to pull defenders out of position.
- If you are a receiver, tell the thrower where to throw the ball – at your feet or chest, down the line or inside.

Technique

Get it right

To avoid a foul throw, which would give possession away, the ball should start behind your head. Keep both your feet on the ground behind the touchline and throw the ball forward, not down.

Receivers should call for the ball and indicate where on their body they want to receive it.

Use this simple throw direct to your team-mate when you are close to your own goal – it's safer.

1 The ball must start from behind your head.

2 Both feet must stay on the floor as you throw.

3 The ball must be thrown forward, not down. Make life easy for the receiver – give him the ball where he wants it. Here the ball is thrown to the receiver's feet.

Practice drill

Using a 15 x 15m grid, one player practises taking a throw-in correctly with a team-mate.

At first the receiver simply controls the ball and returns it to the thrower. Then the players work on this more complex spin routine. It is ideal for losing a marker.

Skills check
- Sound throw-in technique
- Upper-body strength
- Awareness of movement
- Tactical understanding

1 Indicate to the thrower which side you want the ball so that you can spin off.

2 Try to get halfway through your turn before the ball arrives. Cushion it in the air.

3 Then move away out of your spin, with the ball under control, in one fluid movement.

Advanced Move to make space

In this throw-in routine, three attackers make runs, taking their markers with them, to create space for the throw. One striker triggers the move with a decoy run, sprinting in then spinning away from the thrower. The other two make crossover runs along the touchline to confuse the opposition.

Striker B loses his marker and races down the touchline (above). The thrower accurately delivers the ball into his path. Now the attack is on.

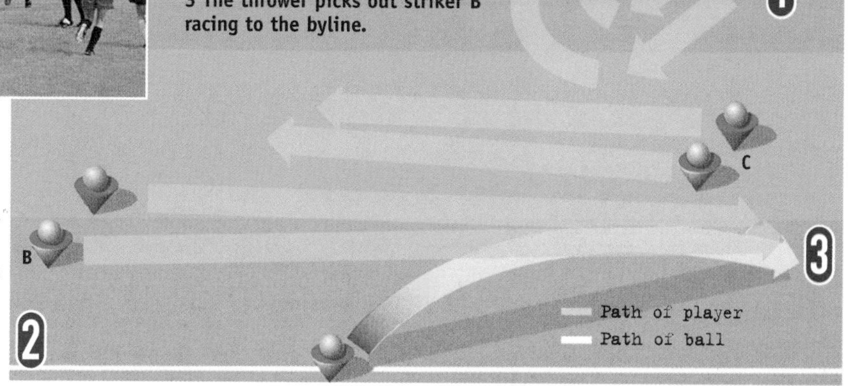

Direct free kicks

A direct free kick is awarded against a player for a serious offence, like a deliberate foul. Less serious offences may incur an indirect free kick. A goal can be scored with a single strike from a direct free kick, so it is well worth trying if you are in range. The position of the keeper and the defensive wall will affect your options.

Skills check
- Accuracy and timing
- Ability to swerve the ball
- Power
- Confidence

Basics Choose your strike

Winning a direct free kick near the penalty area gives you several options:
(1) Swerve your shot around the wall – aiming for the near post.
(2) Chip the ball over the wall with enough dip to bring it below the bar.
(3) Drive the ball low and wide of the wall.
(4) Swerve a shot around the wall – aiming for the far top corner.
(5) Lay the ball off to a team-mate in a better position to score. Try practising this option with your team-mates in a variety of positions.

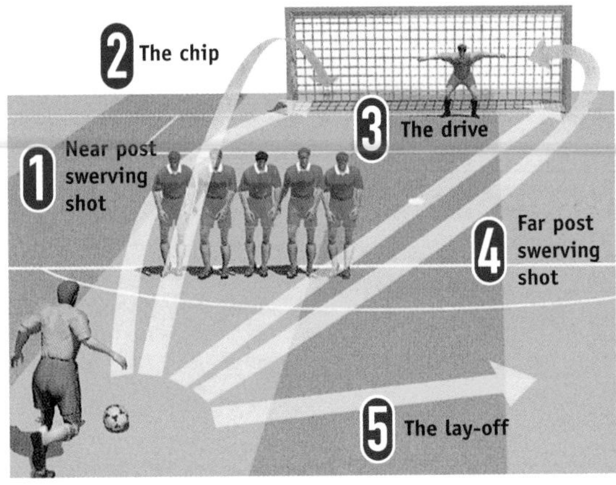

Technique Swerve and power

The basic shot (number 4 above) is a curled strike around the wall with the inside of the foot. As the keeper will expect this, add power to your shot and make sure it is accurate.

With your eye on the ball, keep your balance, planting your non-kicking foot beside the ball.

Once you have mastered the technique, try curling your free kicks around a wall of four of your team-mates. Practise with both feet so that you are sure of yourself wherever the kick is awarded.

1 Approaching the ball from an angled run will give you more leverage to help you gain power.

2 Spin the ball by curling your foot around it. Strike the outside of the ball with the inside of your foot.

3 Following through with your kicking leg helps to ensure that you are using the correct technique.

Indirect free kicks

An indirect free kick is awarded against a player who commits a minor offence – such as obstruction or dangerous play. A goal cannot be scored with a single strike from an indirect free kick – at least two players must get a touch.

Remember, the more complicated the move, the more likely it is to go wrong – simple is usually best.

Skills check
- Organisation
- Imagination
- Decision-making
- Lots of practice on the training ground

Basics Get to goal

Make sure your team have practised all your indirect free kick routines thoroughly before you play a match. Three basic options are shown below, but you can always experiment with others. Always have at least two men over the ball. If the wall has not formed properly, one of the players may want to tap the ball to the other to get a quick strike in at goal.

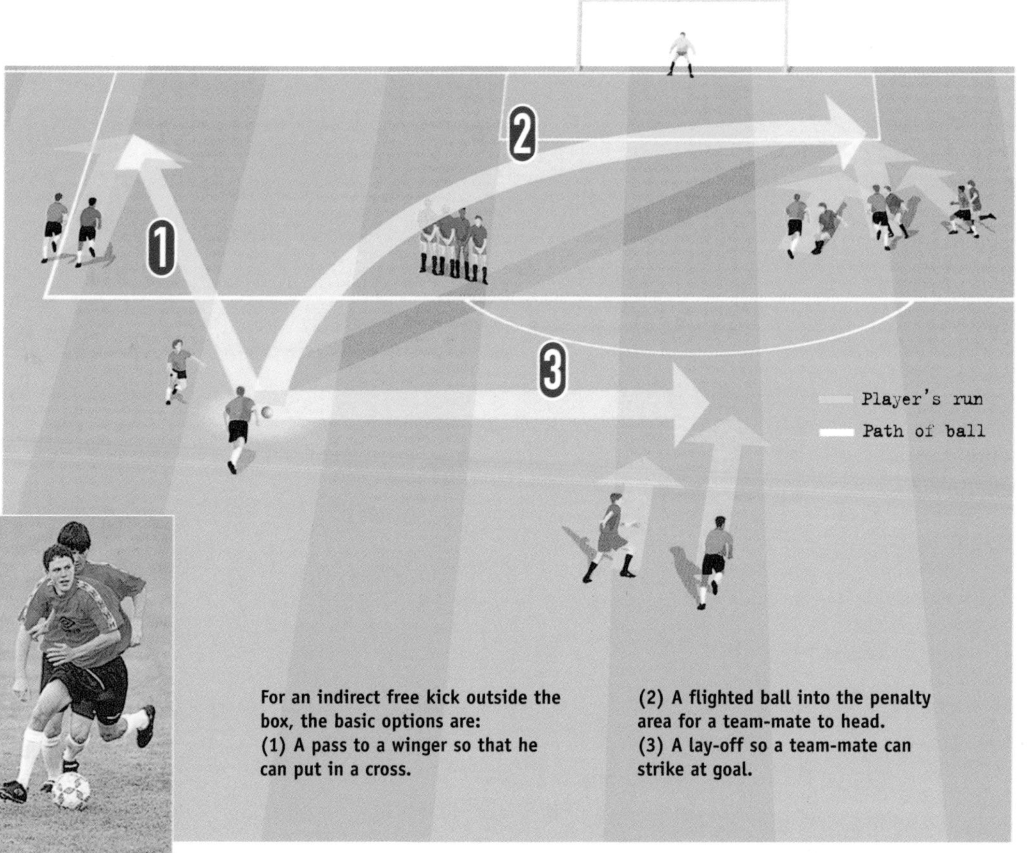

For an indirect free kick outside the box, the basic options are:
(1) A pass to a winger so that he can put in a cross.
(2) A flighted ball into the penalty area for a team-mate to head.
(3) A lay-off so a team-mate can strike at goal.

The inswinging corner

An inswinging corner hit with pace and spin is one of the hardest balls to defend in football. As the ball curls towards goal, it needs only a touch to be diverted on target, giving the keeper little time to react.

To make the most of the corner, choose a left-footed crosser of the ball for corners on the left, and vice versa.

Skills check

- Quality delivery
- Movement off the ball
- Heading ability to finish
- Team co-ordination

Basics Swing near, swing far

The corner taker must ensure the ball is not within the keeper's reach, so he should keep it out of the part of the six-yard box that is directly in front of goal. There are three prime target areas, as shown. If he goes for the far post, the ball must be high enough to evade the defence.

FAR POST
Attackers making late runs from further back can read the flight of the ball and climb higher on the run.

CENTRE AREA
Called the 'second six-yard box', attackers can score from here with just a slight contact on the ball.

NEAR POST
Inswingers aimed in this area require well timed runs for a header on goal, or a flick on across goal.

Practice drill

This near-post inswinging corner routine relies upon accurate delivery of the ball, well-timed attacking runs and heading ability. In the drill, seven attackers play seven defenders and a keeper. The attackers in the penalty area should make runs to gain a vital yard on their markers.

1 The kicker signals a near-post ball.

2 He sends the ball in at pace with spin, aiming inside the six-yard box in line with the near post.

3 The attackers meet the ball at pace.

The near-post corner

One of the most effective tactics you can use at a corner is playing the ball towards the post nearest to you. A ball delivered quickly and at head height close to that post creates confusion among the defence as they try to meet the ball. Additionally, the goalkeeper may come off his line, leaving the goal unguarded.

Skills check
- Accurate delivery at pace
- Sharp movement
- Well timed runs

Basics Signal your delivery

Even before a corner is taken, you can get the edge on your opponents. By designing different corner routines with a variety of runs, decoys and deliveries, your team knows exactly what is going to happen – while your opponents do not. Try having two kickers at a corner so the opposition defence won't know whether to expect a left- or right-footed delivery.

1 Attacker A's raised arm indicates a near-post ball hit by attacker B. (An ear tug could mean a far-post ball.)

2 Both attackers approach the ball to confuse the opposition defence, but attacker A's movement is a decoy.

3 Attacker B actually hits the ball with his right foot – an outswinging corner aimed towards the near post.

Practice drill

One of the most deadly ploys at a near-post corner is for the receiver to flick the ball on rather than head at goal.

By diverting the flight of the ball, you can confuse the keeper and defenders and put the ball right into the danger zone in front of goal.

And if the flick-on is signalled beforehand, your team-mates will know to attack this area and score a goal.

1 Having given a signal to indicate the flick-on move, the corner taker (A) hits the ball, aiming at the near post.

2 The targeted striker (B) gets to the ball first and flicks it on over his marker into the danger zone in front of goal.

3 With the defence and keeper wrong-footed, the second attacker (C) meets the flick-on and directs a header at goal.

Defending against corners

Although many goals are scored from corners, a good team can still do a great deal to defend against them. And a strong clearing header or punch from the keeper can quickly turn defence into counter-attack.

Defending against corners depends on organisation, with each defender in a clearly-defined role.

Skills check
- Good concentration
- Intelligent organisation
- Excellent awareness
- Quick reactions
- Powerful heading

Basics Get organised and concentrate

There are certain details that defending sides should always attend to when trying to clear the ball at corners.

Firstly they should put pressure on the corner taker to stop him playing the ball in well. Secondly they should position men on the posts to cover the keeper, and thirdly they should get the keeper to attack the ball when possible, reaching over the attackers' heads to catch or punch the ball.

PUT ON PRESSURE
One defender pressurises the kicker. He must stay 10 yards away but can jump to try to block the ball.

PROTECT THE GOAL
Two players at each post provide goal-line cover – a second line of defence behind the keeper.

TAKE CHARGE
The keeper must make sure he deals decisively with any ball immediately in front of his goal.

Practice drill

There are two ways to defend at corners – man-to-man or zonal. Most teams operate man-to-man with each defender picking up an attacker. With the zonal method, each defender is responsible for an area of the box, covering all the danger areas.

The purpose of this drill is to practise both defensive approaches. Make sure you have an equal number of attackers and defenders. The attacking team should vary their corners – inswinging and outswinging, near and far post.

MAN-TO-MAN MARKING
Each red defender picks up an attacker and stays goalside of him, looking to beat him to the incoming ball. Tall defenders should mark tall attackers.

ZONAL MARKING
Each red defender is responsible for a three-yard area in front of him. They watch the ball coming over and stay in position to clear the ball if it reaches their zone.

Taking a penalty

Penalties – free shots at goal from the spot 12 yards out – are awarded for fouls in the box, usually because a shot on goal has been prevented. So many competitions are now decided by penalty shoot-outs that it's essential for every player, even the keeper, to take penalties well. Spot kicks are opportunities not to be missed.

Skills check

- Calmness under pressure
- Decisiveness
- Confidence
- Accurate placing
- Powerful shooting

Basics Make a choice

Before you take a penalty, decide whether to use placement or power. If you have a fierce shot, go for power. If you are an accurate passer, place the ball away from the keeper.

The best area for placement is the yellow zone. The purple zone is out of the goalkeeper's reach, but you might send the ball high or wide. For power, try to hit the pale orange zone.

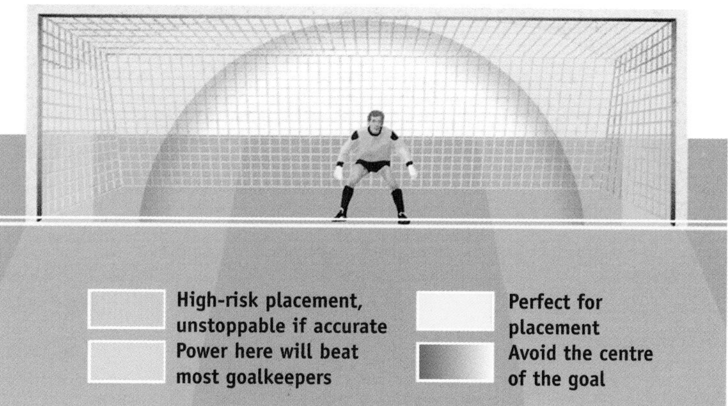

Practice drill

Practise taking penalties in front of a full-size goal with a team-mate. Each time you take a penalty, imagine the result of a match depends on your kick – this might help you deal with the pressure. Attempt both placed and powered strikes and then make up your mind which you are better off using in a match. Remember that confidence is the key: if you think you are going to miss a penalty, you probably will.

Place the shot

Use the side of your foot for the place technique. It keeps the ball lower and improves accuracy.

Power the shot

For power, strike the ball hard with your instep – along the bootlaces.

Part 3

FITNESS

Get to grips with warming-up, plus build up your strength and stamina, to make the most of your soccer matches.

Exercise dos and don'ts

Injuries affect team selection and can decide the fate of matches, trophies, even championships. But they affect individual players the most. A long-term injury can ruin an entire career.

Good fitness training can cut down on injuries, and help to speed recovery when they occur. Conversely, poor fitness training can actually cause injuries.

Use your head

Some exercises that have been part of soccer training for years are now recognised to be potentially dangerous and ought not to be used.

Common sense is often a good guide. Anything that involves bending your joints too far or against the way they want to go puts a strain on them and should be avoided.

Coach says

- **Always make sure you warm up and cool down properly. This greatly reduces your chances of muscle damage.**
- **Don't rush back into training from minor injuries, you could make them long-term problems. Wait until you are healed before restarting.**
- **Be aware of your limits. Don't overdo it.**

Basics Learn the principles

It is surprising how many dangerous and potentially damaging exercises are still performed on football training grounds.

Understanding the reasons why certain stretches and exercises are bad for you will help you identify other potentially dangerous exercises. If you are in any doubt, the safest option is to just steer clear of them.

THE BUNNY HOP

Bunny hops are designed to build explosive power in your legs. Performed poorly, they simply damage your knee joints. Never start on your toes; ensure your knees are at an angle of more than 90°; start and finish on the soles of your feet and throw your arms up as you jump to get maximum distance.

Skills check

- **Strong, supple joints**
- **Explosive pace**
- **Staying power**

THE WINDMILL

Windmills are intended to stretch the leg and stomach muscles. Performing them bent over with arms circling at high speed is bad for your back. Slow your arms and sit down to ensure that your spine is properly supported.

THE HURDLE STRETCH

The classic hurdle stretch, with one leg behind you, puts pressure on your knee ligaments. Instead, pull the leg in front of you so that it touches your leading leg. Reach forward from the waist to your ankle to stretch your hamstring.

THE SPINE STRETCH

Stretching your spine back-to-back can damage the vertebrae by bending them in an unnatural direction. In this safer upright stance the weight of your legs pulls the spine downwards and aids your flexibility.

Body works

Soccer is a contact sport and injuries are therefore inevitable. Take a look at any club's injury list and you will mostly find players recovering from problems in the areas outlined below.

Neck:
Damage can occur to the joints after a heavy or awkward fall. Goalkeepers are most vulnerable to this.

Lower back:
The lower back is especially vulnerable to the rigours of tackling and running.

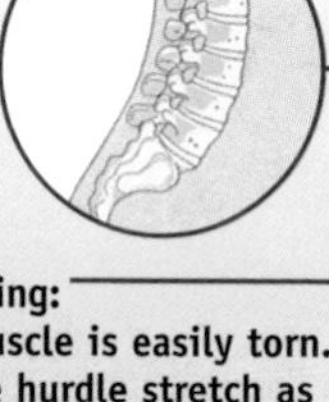

Groin:
The groin muscle can tear, but the bunny hop exercise increases your leg strength, making you less prone to injury.

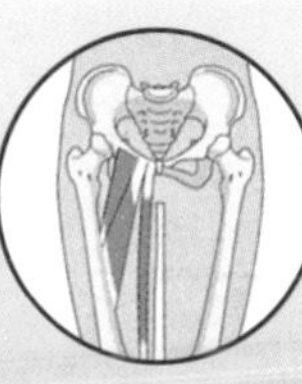

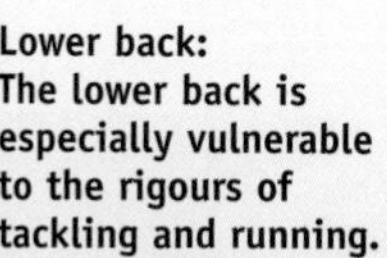

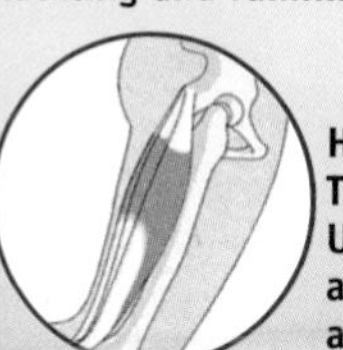

Hamstring:
This muscle is easily torn. Use the hurdle stretch as a cool-down exercise to avoid damage.

Knee:
This complex and sensitive joint is often put under stress from tackling and running.

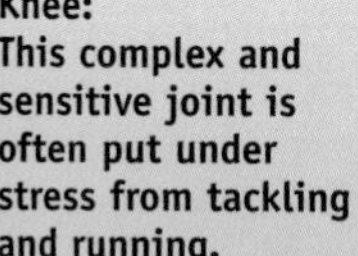

Ankle:
This joint is susceptible to injury sustained in tackles.

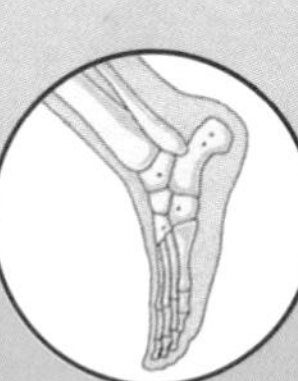

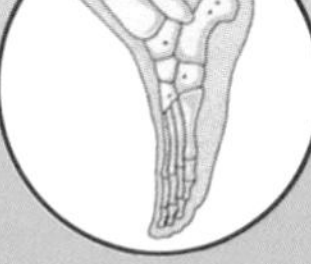

Warm-ups and cool-downs

Matches can be won or lost before the game starts – in the team warm-ups. From the moment the whistle blows, players can be chasing to get in a vital tackle, sprinting on to a through-ball or leaping above an attacker to make a clearance. They will only be ready and able to do it if they are properly warmed up.

About 25 minutes of warm-up is all that is necessary – to get the heart and lungs working and the muscles warm and relaxed.

After the match

Cooling down properly after hard exercise is important. Gentle exercises help the body recover and prevent soreness and stiffness. In the long run this means fewer injuries and fresher players.

Coach says

- Proper warm-ups and cool-downs will mean fewer injuries.
- Flexibility exercises increase your overall performance.

Skills check

- Self-discipline
- Patience
- Concentration
- Positive attitude

Basics Start and finish gently

The first two stages of the warm-up prepare you for action and help you cool down after it. Stage one gets you mobile. In stage two, five minutes of gentle aerobic work gets the blood flowing and raises your muscle temperature – essential in preventing injury.

When used for cooling down, both help your muscles to recover more quickly.

MOVING JOINTS
Begin with slow circular movements of all your joints, first in one direction and then the other: ankles, then knees, hips (above), wrists, elbows and shoulders. The neck should only be moved in semi-circles. This gets all your joints moving smoothly.

GENTLE AEROBICS
Move on to some gentle aerobic work – jogging, passing and 'flex runs' such as the *carioca*, so called because they help flexibility. Move sideways quickly along a line by crossing one leg behind, then in front of you (see above photo).

Body works

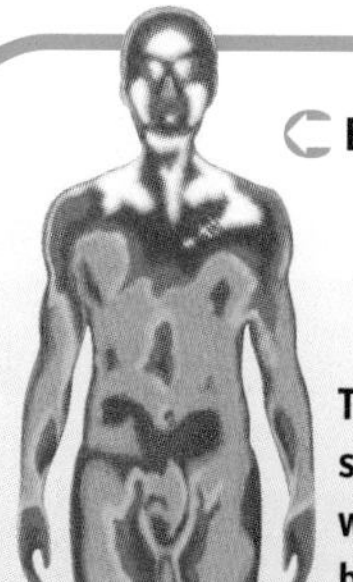

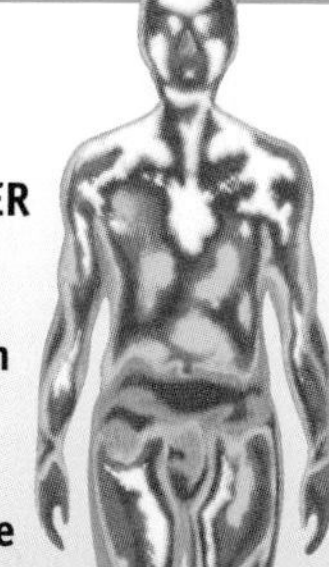

BODY AT REST

BODY AFTER WARM-UP

This thermograph shows how the warm-up affects body temperature

- Body warm
- Brain alert
- Lungs working harder
- Heart rate up
- Muscles warm and relaxed

The body goes through important changes during warming up and cooling down. These prepare the muscles for the intense demands to be placed on them and aid their recovery. This time bar shows how to get the very best out of yourself and recover as swiftly as possible.

Warm-up / *Cool-down*

2 mins moving joints (left)	5 mins gentle aerobics (left)	3 mins dynamic stretches (below)	5 mins fast striding runs	10 mins jumping, heading, shooting	5 mins ready for the match	The match	5 mins easy aerobic work	10 mins static stretches	3 mins legs in the air	10 mins cool shower or bath

Advanced Prepare for speed

The third stage of the warm-up is devoted to dynamic stretching movements. These improve co-ordination and speed, as the brain's nerve pathways are made ready for the fast movements to come in training or a match.

These upper and lower body stretches improve the performance of the muscles that will be used and tested most in a match: the hamstrings, the groin, the back, the chest and the shoulders. These all come into play when sprinting, shooting and tackling, as well as being used for balance and turning quickly. The stretches also work aerobically to get the heart and lungs working more efficiently. Do these for about three minutes.

1 Stand up straight, head still. Hold a hand up to the side of you, then swing your leg up to touch it. Lean on a partner for support.

2 Stand still. Hold your arms in front of you, elbows bent, one above the other. Swing them round behind you to slap your back.

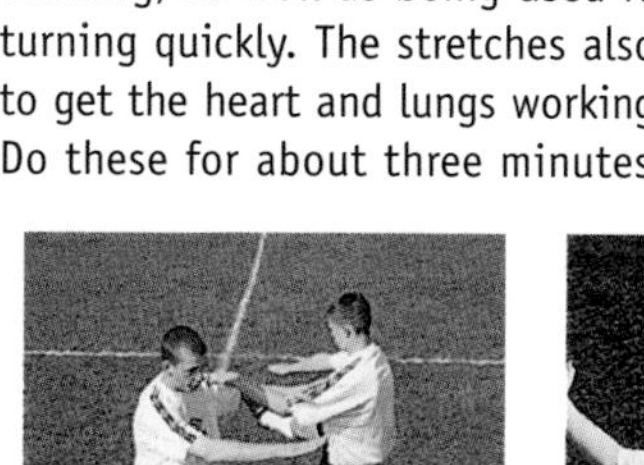

3 Stand up straight, with head still. Hold a hand up in front of you. Don't move your leg back. Swing it up to touch your outstretched hand.

4 Stand still. Hold your arms in front of you in a hugging position. Fling them out backwards so they reach behind you.

Basic stretches

Stretching your muscles thoroughly before both training and matches is vital – both to avoid injuries and to improve performance. Research has shown that a person with stretched muscles can run faster, jump higher and kick farther than an unprepared person. When doing warm-up stretching before playing football, try to cover as many muscles as possible, paying particular attention to the legs.

Stretching sense

When doing any basic stretch, stop and hold your position when you feel a slight strain on the muscle – do not push it any further. Hold for about five to 10 seconds, then slowly release. Shake the muscle loose again so it is relaxed, then repeat the stretch. Now see if you can reach a little further than you did previously, but *don't* overstretch.

Coach says

- **Good stretches as part of your warm-up can make a world of difference to your performance – and they can help reduce the risk of injury.**
- **Don't put too much strain on your muscles – use your common sense to know when to stop.**
- **Don't forget to use stretches as part of your cool-down routine.**

Basics Brace yourself

The calf muscle is very important for the soccer player. Powerful players always have strong calf muscles.

To stretch the calf, brace yourself against a team-mate (right) or a wall. Lean forward with one leg bent in front. Push the other leg straight behind you until you feel a slight strain on the calf. Hold for about 10 seconds.

Skills check

- **Strong, supple joints**
- **All-round performance**
- **Patience**
- **Common sense**

CALF MUSCLE
Try to make your back heel touch the ground, but don't force it.

Flexibility Turn your ankles

The ankle is a very complicated area of the body, and unfortunately this means that there are many things in it that can go wrong.

Increase your flexibility and ankle strength with this simple exercise (right). Standing on one leg (lean on a team-mate if you need to), hold the other leg straight out in front of you. Flex your foot and turn it in slow circles, first clockwise and then anticlockwise.

ANKLE LIGAMENTS Make sure all your movements remain slow and fluid as jerking movements cause unnecessary strain.

Advanced Groin stretching

The groin is an area which is often injured in football. Stretching it well not only reduces this risk, but also increases your mobility. Sit on the floor with your knees bent and lean back on your hands. Slowly push one leg in and downward until you feel a little strain along your thigh. Hold in this position for five to 10 seconds and release gently.

Repeat five times on each leg.

Upper leg and hip stretches

Flexibility and mobility in the upper leg are essential for speed and for skilful play. You start to lose natural mobility and flexibility from the age of eight, so all players need to work on it.

Mobility means how much movement your joints will allow, and flexibility is the potential of the muscles to stretch as you move.

Skills check
- Sprint faster
- Perform skills with more fluency
- Make saving tackles
- Achieve better balance

Flexibility Stretch your legs

Flexibility exercises increase the stretching potential of the muscles, improving movement. The exercises shown here stretch the hamstrings, thigh muscles (quadriceps) and buttock muscles (glutes). Be sure to stretch both legs equally.

Warm up first with five minutes' jogging, then do the stretches slowly and gently, holding each one for 30-60 seconds. Stop if you feel any pain.

HAMSTRING STRETCH Straighten one leg in Front of you. Place both your hands on the opposite thigh and sit back gently. Change legs.

THIGH STRETCH Balance yourself on one leg, slightly bending your knee. Pull your other leg up behind you and hold. Change legs.

BUTTOCK STRETCH Cross one leg over the other. Use the lower leg to pull the crossed leg gently towards your chest. Change legs.

Mobility Swing your hips

Good mobility of the hip joint is essential for sprinting, tackling and turning. If necessary, use a friend for balance as you perform these exercises, and keep your movements smooth and fluid.

1 Keeping your upper body still, swing one leg as far as it will go to one side...

2 ...then swing it across your body as far as you can. Repeat five times and change legs.

1 Again keeping your upper body still, bend the knee to 90° and bring the leg up behind you...

2 ...then swing it up in front of you, keeping the knee bent. Repeat five times on each leg.

Torso stretches

The torso is the centre of power and movement. Mobility and flexibility in this area is vital for players in all positions in a team. When a striker leaps to meet a cross in the penalty area, or a keeper springs to save a shot bound for the top corner, it is their ability to twist and stretch their torsos in mid-air that gives them an extra advantage.

Skills check

- Add direction and power to your headers
- Launch giant throw-ins
- Goalkeepers can make leaping saves

Flexibility Get a front, back and sides

These exercises stretch the muscles at the front, back and sides of your torso. It is important for all soccer players to lengthen and make these muscles more elastic, especially after strength training exercises, which have the effect of shortening the muscles.

TUMMY STRETCH
Lie on your back and stretch as far as you can. Point your toes forwards and reach with your fingers backwards. Hold for 30 seconds.

BACK STRETCH
Bend your knees. Arch your spine and drop your head slowly – don't move jerkily – to let your arms hang. Hold for 30 seconds.

SIDE STRETCH
Reach one hand up and slide the other hand slowly down the opposite thigh as you bend. Stop if you feel any pain. Keep your hips still and weight evenly balanced between both feet.

Mobility Put your back into it

These exercises help to improve the mobility of the joints and discs of the lower and middle sections of the spine. The first exercise improves your ability to bend to the side. The second increases your ability to twist from the waist. Do each for 30 seconds to one minute at a time.

With your arms up and your hips still, bend gently down from side to side.

Keep your hips still and twist gently from the waist. Move from side to side.

Increase your speed

Skills check
- ○ Good running action
- ○ Muscle power
- ○ Determination

Whether it's over a distance of five or 50 yards, speed is crucial in football. In a race for the ball between a striker and a defender, pace makes all the difference between winning and losing possession.

And when launching a counter attack, players must cover virtually the entire length of the pitch at top speed.

Basics Perfect the body action

To increase your speed it is vital to use the correct sprinting action. Practise the technique and keep testing its effectiveness by timing your training runs – first over 25m, then 50m. Remember to do a thorough warm-up first, especially focusing on the leg muscles.

First practise the arm action. With your elbows bent, pump your arms from ear to hips. Start slowly to get the action right, then speed up.

For the leg action, lift each knee up so that the thigh is horizontal to the ground. Drag your studs back along the turf as your foot lands.

Put the action into practice by stepping into the spaces of a rope ladder at speed.

Advanced Move sideways at speed

During a game, the ability to move sideways quickly is as crucial as running forwards at speed.

Practise lateral movement by setting up two rows of hurdles about 3m apart. Run to the first hurdle on the right row and place your right foot over it. Push off from this foot and accelerate across to the first hurdle on the left row. Continue zig-zagging your way down the course.

Try varying your pace – speed up at the right row and slow down at the left.

Run to the first hurdle and plant your outside foot over it.

Push off from this outside foot and speed away to the next hurdle.

Repeat the action on the next hurdle.

Sprinting exercises

During a match, there will be lots of occasions when opponents race against each other to get to the ball first. Every player can improve his speed by working on technique, strength and endurance, and explosive power. To sprint faster in a game – and win the ball more often – you must learn to sprint faster in training.

Skills check
- Lose markers
- Be first to loose balls
- Run on to through passes
- Move into space
- Counter-attack at pace
- Cover quickly

Basics Keep your knees high

Try fast stepping with high knees. Put markers out as in the diagram. For the first 4m, get in as many fast high steps as you can. As you reach the first marker, burst forward and sprint the last 15m.

Try to maintain the bounce of the high knees section into the sprint section. Drive your elbows back so that your knees come through more quickly.

Keep your legs moving quickly as you lengthen your stride. Relax and try not to bend forward from the waist.

Advanced Catch him if you can

Tag sprints are great fun and perfect for building explosive speed. In this drill for four people, the standing players have to 'tag' their partners – sitting or lying down 3m away – before they can jump up and get to the finishing line 10m further on.

All the sprinters start at the same time. The players on the ground must get into a starting position in one movement – pushing up and getting their best foot forward. They should be sprinting away before they have fully straightened up, like an Olympic 100m runner coming out of the blocks. The chasers must concentrate on starting quickly and maintaining good technique – focusing too much on the player ahead can slow the chaser down.

1 The standing sprinters must make up 3m on their partners.

2 All the sprinters start together. The finishing line is 10m further on.

Use your top speed

Learning to relax and use your top speed is an essential part of modern football. The rise of counter-attacking sides means that long sprints are frequent, and fast players have an advantage.

Even the keeper must learn to develop top speed. He may have to race from his area to clear the ball, then chase back to his line.

Skills check

- Breaking forward quickly
- Tracking back at speed
- Running on to long balls
- Getting back into position after clearances outside the penalty box

Basics Try cruise control

Relaxing, even at top speed, is the key to running faster. In this 'switch-off' drill, you accelerate gradually and try to hit top speed as you reach the 10m mark.

You then stop trying to accelerate, but keep working your arms and legs for the next 20m. Amazingly, the expected sudden slowdown doesn't happen. You will still be gliding quickly, using hardly any effort.

This exercise produces an amazing sensation – as you learn to glide at top speed, you will be flying along in perfect relaxation.

0m Power on 10m Switch off 30m

Practice drill

20 m
10 m
20 m

The players 'glide' at speed through the middle 10m section then put on the power and try to accelerate again for the last 20m

Staying relaxed and maintaining a good sprint technique is vital for top speed.

This 20m-10m-20m drill aims to build on the principle of relaxation to develop maximum speed for the frequent long sprints in a game.

The first 20m section is run flat out, the middle 10m is performed as in the switch-off run, gliding at speed. Then, in the final 20m, the players switch the power back on but remain relaxed.

Learning to accelerate again after gliding can help produce the vital extra speed that could leave your opponents trailing in your wake.

Skills at speed

Football gets faster and faster. As you progress to new levels of the game, you get less time on the ball, less time to control it, less time to shoot. Judging the pace of a game can be the hardest part of it.

The skills used in every game, from simple turns to acrobatic volleys, all require great balance, co-ordination and awareness – often at speed.

Skills check

- Dribbling
- Ball control
- Passing
- Awareness
- Balance

Basics Dribble through danger

This drill helps your individual ball control. You must keep control of the ball and avoid the other players.

Players form a queue of two or more at each corner of a 10m square. Two dribble diagonally to their opposite corners where the facing player collects the ball and dribbles back. If the drill breaks down, just collect the ball and keep going.

Advanced Run, pass and spin

This drill tests your ability to recover from a disorienting spin in time to receive and release a pass.

Players line up at a corner of a 10m square, with four passers inside the square. Players run along the outside of the grid, collect and return a pass, turn through 360° at the next corner, and repeat on each side. When a player reaches the first corner, the next one begins.

1 Set off along the grid. At the halfway point, collect and return the pass from a player in the centre.

2 At the corner, turn through 360°, then run on to meet the next pass.

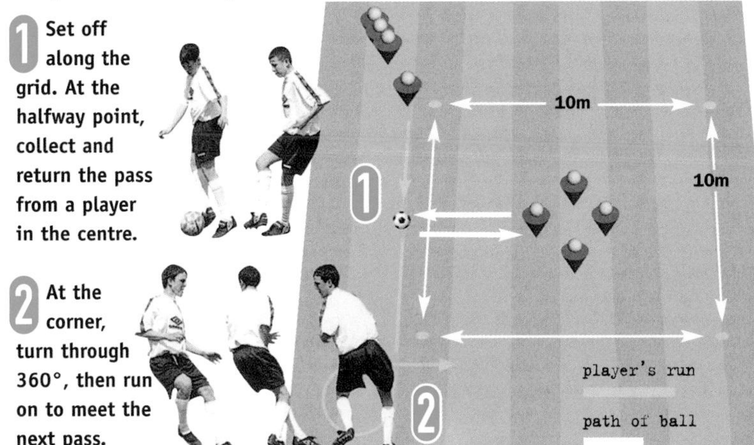

Increase your endurance

To perform at your best, from kick-off to final whistle, it is essential to have a high level of endurance. This is particularly true in today's game, with football becoming ever more demanding.

Endurance, or stamina, is particularly important during the final quarter of a match, when games are often won and lost.

Skills check
- Pressurising opponents
- Making runs
- Performance throughout a match

Basics Give your heart a workout

You can build endurance by running at a regular pace until you get out of breath.

Try making training more fun by introducing a ball and setting out a dribbling circuit, as shown on the right. Use any design, but make it large enough to give yourself a proper workout. The idea is to get your heart pumping faster for at least 15 minutes. Don't forget to do warm-ups first.

In this drill, the players run from the red markers to the top right corner. They then run in and out of the yellow cones, collect a ball and dribble their way through the blue markers back to the start.

Advanced Train as a team

1 Do step-overs on the hurdles, using the balls of your feet.

2 Next, do body swerves in and out of the cone markers.

3 Then run along the end of the grid while heading and catching a ball.

Training with your team makes endurance work more fun. This advanced drill gets players working on skills around a 20 x 10m grid. The circuit includes hurdles to step over, cones to swerve around, and a heading and catching exercise (shown left).

Try not to let the person behind you catch up; and keep going for as long as you can. When you've got your breath back, try another circuit. After each session, make a note of your best time so that you have a target to beat next time.

Strength exercises

Strength is a must for players in every area of the pitch – from goalkeepers faced by 150km/h shots, to strikers and defenders battling shoulder-to-shoulder. Your level of strength can be improved, and used to advantage.

Strength-building exercises require resistance and the best way to provide this is to use your body weight.

Skills check

- Shielding
- Tackling
- Competing for the ball
- Saving hard shots

Basics Build whole-body strength

Combining these individual exercises builds up your whole-body strength. Press-ups build arm, shoulder and stomach muscles. Step-ups build hamstrings, quadruceps and groin muscles. Squats build up your legs, back and stomach muscles.

All you will need is a sturdy box. Work slowly up to three sets of 10 on each individual exercise.

PRESS-UPS
Keep your head up and your body straight as you lower yourself. Breathe in as you go down; out on the way up. Repeat five times.

STEP-UPS
Put one foot on the box, step up with one foot, then step down. Do 10; swap feet and repeat.

SQUATS
From upright, sink down slowly into the squat with your arms out, then come up slowly. Repeat 10 times.

Safety zone

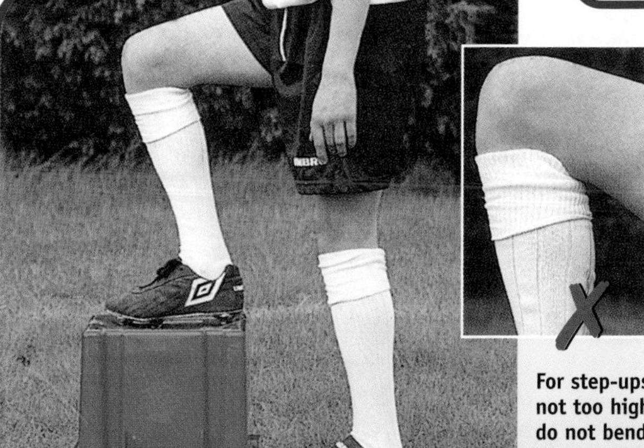

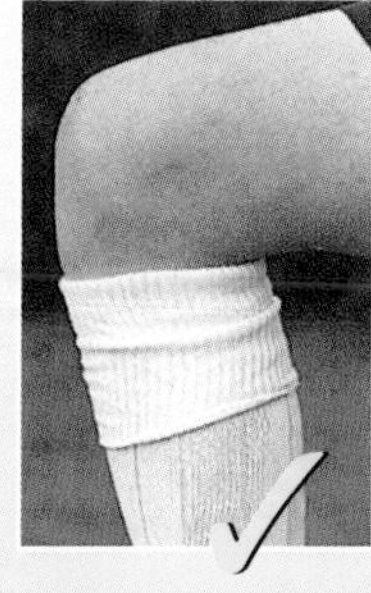

For step-ups, make sure the box is not too high, so that your knees do not bend more than 90° as you step up. For squats, don't lower your body below a 90° knee angle.

The knee joint is complicated and easily damaged. This is especially true during growth spurts, when bones are growing quickly, pulling muscles and tendons tighter.

The joint must not be squashed when doing exercises that involve bending the knee. In step-ups or squats, it should not bend more than 90°.

Increase your power

Power is different from strength because it involves speed. Power comes from the legs as much as the arms.

Increasing your power pays a long-term dividend and makes a difference to your performance, wherever you play. Taking throw-ins, turning, shooting, sprinting and jumping can all be improved with added power.

Skills check
- Shooting
- Jumping
- Heading
- Goalkeeping distribution
- Throw-ins
- Sprinting

Basics Toss the caber and twist the pass

These drills use a small, heavy medicine ball, but you can perform them with a normal football.

The first exercise is the caber toss. It helps increase your whole body power and shows how you gain speed by pushing off from your legs and accelerating into the jump. The second exercise is the twist pass which increases power in the twisting muscles in the side of your body.

1 **Crouch down holding the ball in both hands. Bend from your knees, don't go too low.**

2 **Push up from the legs first then explode up. Release the ball as your arms go over your head.**

3 **Throw the ball as high as you can so your feet leave the ground. Repeat five times; rest and repeat.**

1 **Stand side-on facing in different directions. Twist away from your partner to throw the ball.**

2 **Rotate quickly back to launch the ball with power at him. Do it five times each side. Rest and repeat.**

Safety zone

This player is leaning back too far, trying to get full power into his throw. He is arching his back in a dangerous way and is also off balance as he tilts back. ✗

✓ **Here, he is in a perfect position to get power from his legs. He is using his whole body to give his arms extra acceleration.**

To harness your new body power in a match, you must use the correct technique. This reduces the risk of injury.

For throw-ins this involves using the power of your legs and stomach, without overarching your back or losing balance.

Increase your leg power

Virtually every part of your game can be improved by building up your leg power. Strong thigh and calf muscles are obviously needed for sprinting, shooting and jumping – but they also help in changing direction quickly and shielding the ball. Even the keeper needs leg power – to launch into a diving save or sprint out from goal.

Skills check
- Increased shooting power
- Harder tackling
- More explosive pace
- Improved ability to perform skilful turns
- Higher jumping

Basics Jump to it

Jumping exercises such as toe touching and heel flicks can be done in a small space with nothing more than a cardboard box. Work on a fluid jumping motion to limit wasted energy.

Safety zone

Start every leg-power session with some leg stretches to warm up. This will reduce the risk of injury and increase your flexibility. Remember to cool down as well, to relax the muscles. Work on grass and wear football boots or trainers to absorb impact.

Toe touching improves precision leg movements.

TOE TOUCHING
Put the box in front of you. Run on the spot, but on each step touch your toes lightly on the top of the box. This will improve your running technique.

Do 10 heel flicks at a time.

HEEL FLICKS
Stand with your legs on either side of the box. Spring up so that your heels touch each other in the air, then land in your original position.

Advanced Move on to circuit training

Set up the obstacles around the square. Use what you can – plastic plates or flower pots for markers and sticks or rolled-up newspapers to form the quick-foot ladder.

1 Jump over the small markers or plastic plates while gripping a football between your feet.

2 Jump sideways over the hurdles or flower pots, turning to change your leading foot each time.

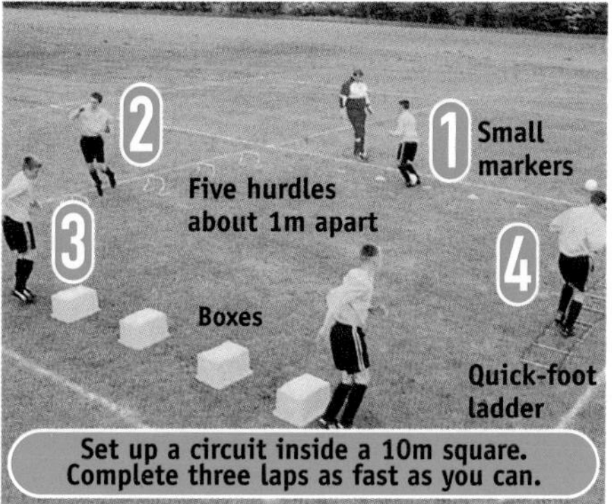

Set up a circuit inside a 10m square. Complete three laps as fast as you can.

Strengthen your weaker side

Some of the world's greatest players have been one-foot wonders, but soccer is increasingly a two-footed sport. All aspects of your game can be improved by strengthening your weaker foot – from shooting and passing, to controlling the ball, dribbling and even tackling.

Build it up

Working on your weaker foot demands determination. You have to be prepared to train hard and then try shots and tackles with your weaker foot in a match – even if you know you can perform better with your stronger one. The more attention you give to your weaker foot, the better it will become.

Coach says

- Two-footedness makes you less vulnerable. Players can't exploit a weakness on one side when they try to go past you, or push you on to your weaker foot when you are going forward.

Skills check

- Ball skills
- Shooting
- Running with the ball
- Tackling
- Turning

Basics Relax and get stronger

The confidence you feel when shooting with your stronger foot comes from years of practice, starting from the time you first kicked a ball.

Building absolute confidence with your weaker foot takes years of practice, too. But these exercises – to increase strength and work on relaxation on your weaker side – will speed up the process. The long-term effect on your versatility will be huge.

AIR SHOTS
Practise shooting with your weaker foot without a ball. This forces you to concentrate on the movement of the body and helps to make it relaxed and flowing. And remember – stay relaxed when you shoot for real.

FORWARD AND LATERAL HOPS
Lay a 10m line of markers with 30cm gaps. Hop over the markers along the line, first forwards (left), then sideways (right) on your best foot. Change feet to come back. This builds balancing strength in both legs

Body works

There is no point wishing to be either left- or right-footed, as you have no control over which side is dominant. It's already decided when you're a baby – but you can still compensate for this.

A brain of two halves

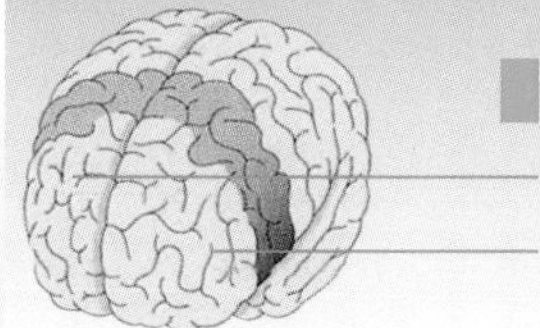

The brain is made up of two linked halves. If the left side becomes dominant. you become right-handed, and vice versa.

0 Newborn baby turns head more to one side than the other.	**6-9 mths** Baby favours one hand to pick up food and toys.	**15 mths** Baby chooses same hand for feeding with spoon.	**2** Toddler uses same foot to kick a football.	**3** Child learns to use both hands for eating with knife and fork.	**5+** Child can be encouraged to kick a ball with both feet. The earlier you practise with your 'wrong' foot, the stronger it will get.
one-sided development				two-sided development	

Advanced Turn and shoot

Test your improved strength and confidence with this practice for up to four players in front of goal. Mark a line 10m away from the goal and place your ball 7m away from the goal. Starting at your ball, you need to: (1) run to the 10m line; (2) turn quickly off your weaker foot and sprint back to the ball; (3) fire it into the net with your weaker foot, using a relaxed and flowing movement.

1

2

3

Increase your agility

Agility is the ability to change direction or position quickly – without losing control of your body. If you can swerve, feint, shimmy and change direction when running at speed, you are agile. Twisting and turning in a crowded penalty area to get a strike in on goal, or out-jumping a defender to reach a cross, both demand great agility.

Beating a challenge

Agility has four basic qualities – speed, strength, balance and co-ordination. Great players have all of these qualities, which allow them to beat defenders and evade close marking. They can bounce out of challenges and remain in control of their body.

Improve your agility by focusing on how you move, and by reducing all unnecessary movement.

Coach says

- Practise dodging obstacles to improve your agility. It will help you perform skilful turns and body swerves.
- Repeat drills again and again to perfect a fluid body action.
- Conserve energy by reducing any unnecessary movement.

Basics Control your body

After your warm-up stretches (Safety Zone, above right) start every agility training session with a walk drill (near right). This will give you greater control over your limbs for the more advanced drills. It will also stretch your muscles. The cross-step (far right) helps to develop your balance.

Skills check

- Speed
- Good timing
- Balance and co-ordination
- Great body control

WALK DRILL
Walk forwards on the balls of your feet taking long strides. Swing your arms and raise your knees up high on each step. Speed up your strides gradually but do not run.

CROSS-STEP
Cross your left foot over your right foot, step to the side with your right, cross your left foot behind it and again step to the side with your right foot. Swap feet; repeat to the left.

Safety zone

Stretching exercises not only increase your flexibility and agility, but also reduce the risk of injury by warming your muscles. Do these exercises before every match or training session.

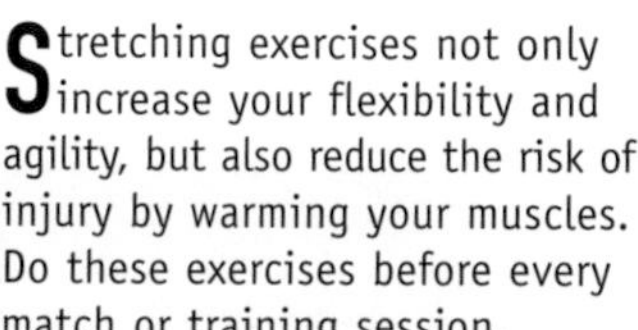

HAMSTRINGS
Sit with your legs together, knees slightly bent. Push your upper body forwards gently.

THE GROIN
Sit upright with the soles of your feet together. Push forwards and squeeze your knees down with your elbows.

Grip your ankles with your hands to maintain balance.

CALF MUSCLES
Lean against a solid support with your back leg extended. Push down on to the heel of your back leg. Repeat with the other leg.

Keep your back straight and your heels on the floor.

Advanced Work in a circuit

Step into and out of each ladder rung space then hurdle the obstacles. Next, jump along the ladder, turning in the air as you jump. And finally, perform the Basics walk drill. (You can use boxes and sticks instead of hurdles and ladders.)

1 LADDER STEP
Put your left foot in the first rung space then your right. Step back out in the same way. Move on to the next space.

2 OBSTACLE JUMP
Jump over the line of obstacles, twisting through 180° each time

3 LADDER JUMP
With feet together, jump from space to space. Twist your body from side to side as you go.

4 WALK DRILL
Do the walk drill (as in Basics, left). At the half-way marker, turn round and perform the drill backwards.

Sharpen your reactions

Fast reactions are a key element in playing good football. In fact, the ability to react with lightning speed can often make the vital difference between success and failure. Split-second reactions are needed in all aspects of the game. Strikers can use them to catch out defences, while keepers need them to make saves.

The right attitude

An ability to react quickly requires both mental and physical sharpness. Training can improve your ability to react quickly, but you also need the right mental attitude. Good anticipation, concentration and determination will all make a vital difference in your reaction times.

Coach says

- **Practise your eye, hand and feet reactions both with and without the ball.**
- **Make reaction training a part of all of your practice sessions.**
- **Practise with a partner. Make the drills a random sequence so that neither of you knows what to expect next.**

Basics Speed up

This drill is designed to improve your reactions, together with your hand, eye and foot co-ordination. It also develops greater body control, speed and ball control.

As with all these drills, do some warm-up stretches before starting the exercise and follow it with a cool-down routine.

Skills check

- **Good awareness**
- **Positive mental attitude**
- **Excellent co-ordination**
- **Good agility**

1 **A player holds two footballs at shoulder height, and then drops one – without indicating to the other player which side it will be.**

2 **The other player must react as quickly as he can, stepping forwar to trap the ball on its first bounce w the foot on that side.**

Practice drill

Four players with a ball each stand in a circle about 5m in diameter. A fifth player stays in the middle.

Nominate a captain to call out the name of any one of the four with a ball. This player promptly throws his ball at head height to the player in the centre, who heads it back as accurately as possible to the thrower.

The drill must be carried out at high speed. Take it in turns to be the middle player and the captain.

React as sharply as possible, but maintain good accuracy

Advanced Improve your all-round vision

This drill develops your all-round vision, known as peripheral vision, which is needed constantly throughout a game.

All players need to be aware of what is happening around them. Awareness helps to assist long-range passing, to avoid falling victim to surprise attacks, to communicate to team-mates what is going on, to help anticipate others' moves and to read the game as it progresses. All players in this drill take 10 turns in the centre.

1 Two players face each other with a third in the middle facing straight ahead. The central player throws a ball into the air.

2 While the first ball is still in the air, a second ball is thrown to the central player by one of the other two.

3 He catches this second ball and throws it to the third player before the first ball drops. The cycle is then repeated.

Balancing exercises

In soccer, there is more to balancing than just staying on your feet. Hitting high volleys demands perfect balance on one leg to control the shot. Dribbling well with the ball requires constant shifting of your weight from one side to the other in order to wrong-foot your opponent. Defensive skills also require good balance.

Skills check

- Stay on your feet
- Shimmy round challenges
- Steady yourself to hit volleys
- Tackle effectively

Basics Keep your balance

These simple exercises strengthen all the muscles that help you to control your balance.

The first helps the nerve endings in the ankle. It is ideal if you have recovered from an ankle injury but don't yet want to put the ankle through a work-out in a match.

The second makes the muscles around the hip work very hard to maintain your balance.

STAND ON ONE FOOT
Put your arms out and balance on one leg with eyes closed for 20 seconds.

THROW AND CATCH
With a partner, play a game of throw and catch. Stand on one leg and toss a football back and forth without losing your balance. Change leg each time you do.

Advanced Walk the thin line

To attempt this balancing exercise, you need a pole, beam or log on the ground. Get some friends to hold it steady.

Raise your arms and set out along the beam. Do not lift your arms midway through the walk – this can actually throw you off balance. Keep your head still and move slowly to allow your brain and muscles to learn how to respond to the difficulties in balancing. Walk as far as you can. Keep trying until you can get to the end.

Try to walk along a pole without falling off. After you've mastered going forwards, try turning around in the middle or walking backwards.

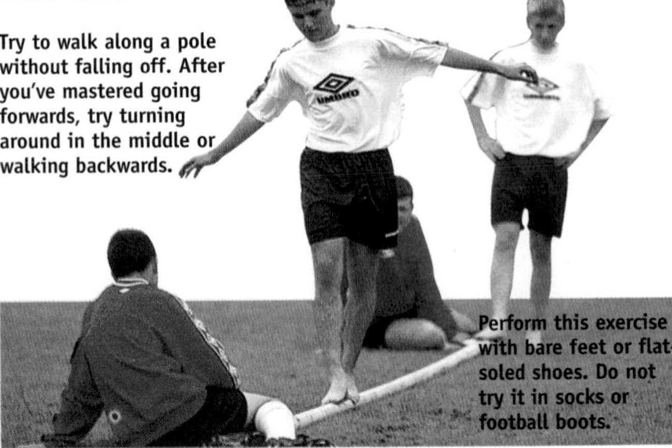

Perform this exercise with bare feet or flat-soled shoes. Do not try it in socks or football boots.

Jumping exercises

Skills check
- Powering off the ground
- Hovering
- Awareness in the air
- Twisting
- Saving high shots

The ability to jump is the key to heading the ball well. If you can't leap high and fast, you can't attack, defend or win the ball in the air. Jumping efficiently also helps you when controlling a high pass with your feet or your chest. And for keepers, leaping is absolutely essential for fielding crosses and saving high shots.

Basics Drive your knees up

Both these exercises improve your jumping ability. The skipping exercise is designed for taking off from one foot. The object is to drive the knees up high. Start slowly and go for height not distance.

In the stride jump, you start on two feet. Get up on your toes and jump off the ground quickly. Try to explode on the upward and outward jump movements.

SKIPPING
Work your arms and legs across a 20m grid. As your arm comes up, let it bring the opposite knee with it as high as possible.

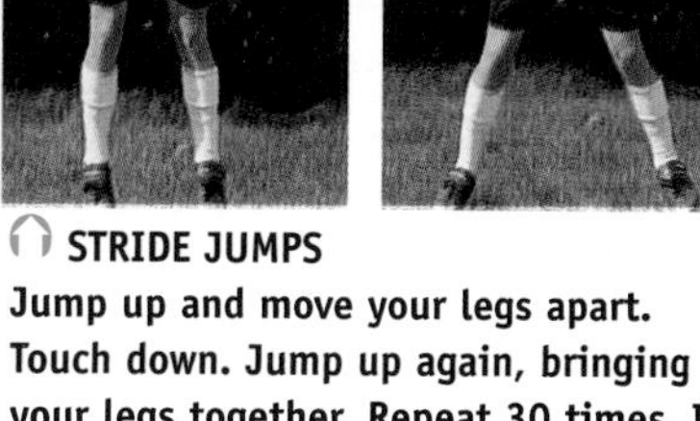

STRIDE JUMPS
Jump up and move your legs apart. Touch down. Jump up again, bringing your legs together. Repeat 30 times. If you want to, introduce arm movements.

Advanced Jump and spin

Compass jumps help you to rotate your body as you jump, essential for heading and competing for the ball in the air.

This drill combines the basic compass jumps into a sequence that will test your concentration and put power into your turning muscles. The key is to keep your legs apart as you jump to get maximum rotation. As you gain confidence, try to do it faster.

1 Jump up and spin 90° to your left while in the air.

2 Jump and spin back to your original position.

3 Jump up again and spin 90° to your right.

4 Jump and spin back to your start position.

5 Jump up and spin through 180° to your left.

6 Jump and spin 180° to your right, back to the start position.

Turning exercises

One good turn can decide a game. Sudden changes of direction take markers by surprise and create space to accelerate clear. They often create a pathway through the defence to goal.

Attackers have to turn quickly to make late runs and beat opponents in one-on-one situations, and defenders must be able to match them.

Skills check
- Change direction
- Beat opponents
- Lose markers
- Run into space
- Go with runners
- Tackle back

Basics Do the zig-zag

Improve your swerving ability by zig-zagging quickly through a set of markers. As you come into each turn, get both feet around the marker to push away strongly out of the turn.

Safety zone

Turn correctly or you may slip and hurt yourself. Don't stretch one leg out. Keep your body low and take short steps. Use two feet to turn.

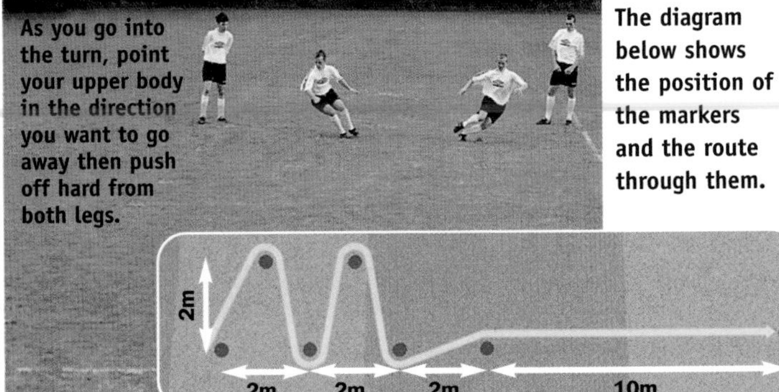

As you go into the turn, point your upper body in the direction you want to go away then push off hard from both legs.

The diagram below shows the position of the markers and the route through them.

Practice drill

Turning at speed can help you lose a close marker or defend against a through-ball. This drill, in which you run for 10m, turn and sprint back 3m, then turn and sprint again, improves your technique and power as you do the turns.

Push off from a crouching start. Sprint hard for 10m.

Turn at the 10m marker. Don't lean out too far, keep your body weight balanced and use two feet to change direction. Sprint back for 3m.

At the third marker turn quickly again, push off and sprint to the end.

Develop explosive pace

Explosive pace comes into play all the time in soccer. It gets you to the ball first to win possession, it takes you away from your marker, and it is what you use to burst past opponents anywhere on the pitch. Fast acceleration gives you the edge in almost every aspect of the game and it needs to be part of your regular training routine.

Skills check
- Natural pace
- Body strength – particularly in the legs
- Good balance

Basics Get up and go

Get-up drills are designed to teach players to be more explosive from a stationary position. Try these two variations and see the difference next time you play in a game.

Always do your warm-up and stretching routine before starting any training drill or exercises. For two people you will need four markers – shoes, bags or sticks will do. Place two markers 1m apart and the other two markers 10m away. Take it in turns to start the drill.

SITTING START

Sit level beside your markers, with your backs to the other two markers. One of you calls 'Go!' You both get up, turn and sprint 10m to the other markers. Try releasing as much power as possible in the first strides. Repeat five times.

PRESS-UP START

This is a harder drill. Start in the press-up position facing the 10m markers. On the call, burst forward and sprint towards the markers. Try facing the other way, too, so you have to get up, turn and sprint. Do each five times.

Body works

Each muscle contains thousands of fibres, each about the size of a human hair. When you tense a muscle, you can feel it harden as these fibres contract.

There are two types of fibres: ones that contract slowly (slow-twitch fibres) and ones that contract quickly – fast-twitch fibres. These are larger and get tired quicker than slow-twitch fibres. They are important when you put on a burst of pace. Sprint training makes the fast-twitch fibres larger still, giving you more explosive power.

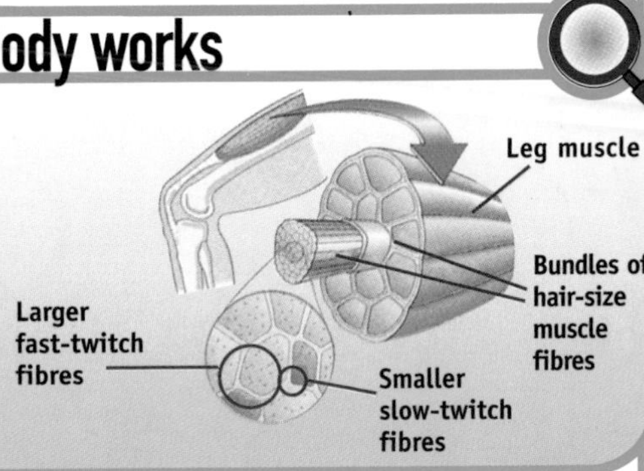

Check speed and power

What is the value of an extra metre of pace for every player in the team? Why is it worth jumping an extra 10cm every time the ball is in the air? Over a season, you might see the difference where it counts – in the goal tallies and in your points total.

Set your fitness targets

Increases in speed and power are fitness goals that can be measured. Over a period of training, you can see not only that you are becoming faster and more powerful, but by exactly how much.

Remember, it's not enough to just play in matches and to hope your speed and power will increase. For maximum impact on the pitch, you need to set yourself realistic fitness goals and work to achieve them.

Coach says

- Warm up and do the tests at the start of a training session.
- Explosive power starts off at maximum and declines if you attempt the same test 20 times in a row.

Skills check

- Explosive pace
- Jumping power
- Straight-line speed

Test one: 30m sprint

Testing your speed and power allows you to judge how much you improve over time. The speed test is a 30m sprint, timed at 5m, 10m and 30m to check explosive pace, acceleration and speed. Get a friend to test you each week, with a stop watch or a watch that has a second hand.

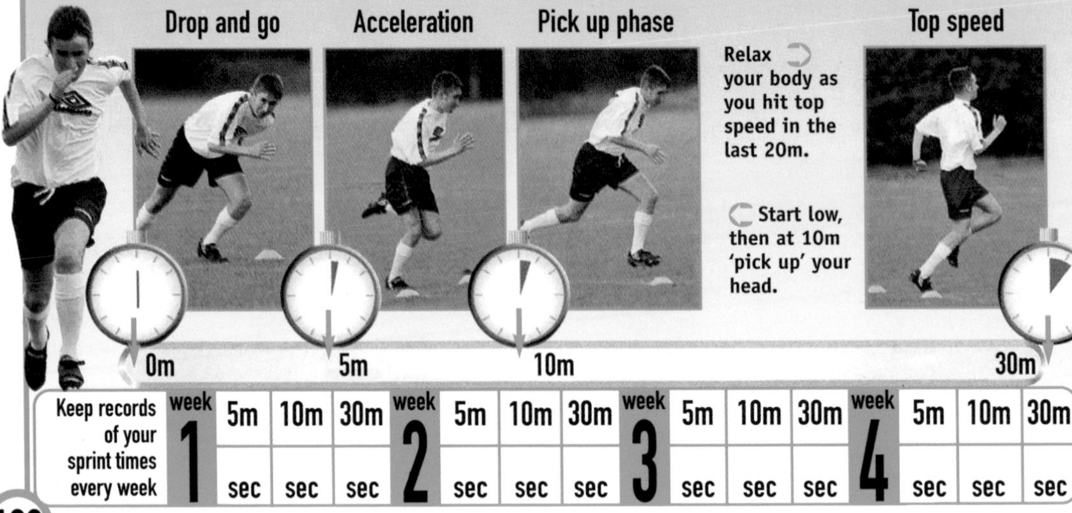

Relax your body as you hit top speed in the last 20m.

Start low, then at 10m 'pick up' your head.

Keep records of your sprint times every week															
	week 1	5m	10m	30m	week 2	5m	10m	30m	week 3	5m	10m	30m	week 4	5m	10m	30m
		sec	sec	sec		sec	sec	sec		sec	sec	sec		sec	sec	sec

Test two: standing jump

As an indicator of you explosive power, measure how far you can jump.

From a standing start, bend your legs to give yourself spring and try to land on your soles. Note down your best jump of five attempts each week.

Start from a line
Throw your arms up

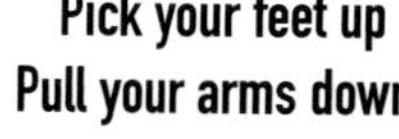

Pick your feet up
Pull your arms down

Measure the distance
with a tape measure

0m — 1m — 2m

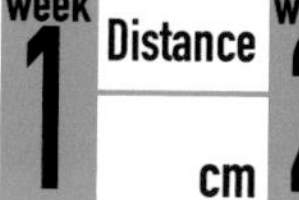

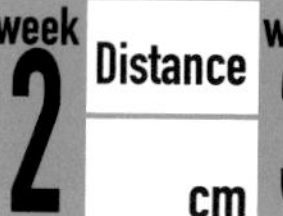

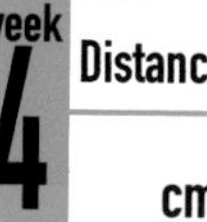

Keep records of your jumps every week	week 1	Distance	week 2	Distance	week 3	Distance	week 4	Distance
		cm		cm		cm		cm

Test three: vertical jump

Jumping high helps your heading ability. These tests measure how high you can jump from standing. Bend your knees to spring up and reach up with one hand.

Measure how high you can reach up a goalpost or a wall. Then jump as high as you can and mark how high you can touch. Subtract the first figure from the second to work out how high you managed to jump off the ground.

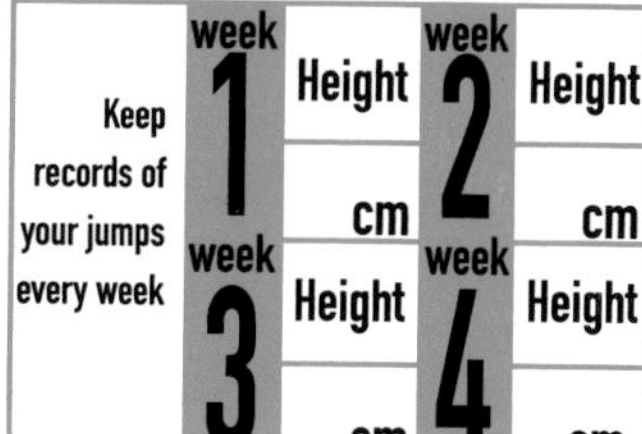

Keep records of your jumps every week	week 1	Height	week 2	Height
		cm		cm
	week 3	Height	week 4	Height
		cm		cm

Insight: Outrun your friends

Some speed and power is inherited, but you can always build on what you are born with. By challenging your friends to regular running races and jumping contests, you will be motivated to improve your performance.

Get a friend to time the races and measure your jumps. That way you can monitor your own improvement in speed as well as your competitive performance against your friends.

Imagine if, by working on your speed and power, you could become the fastest and most athletic among your friends. What a fantastic confidence boost!

INDEX

DIMENSIONS OF THE PITCH

1 yard = 0.91 metres

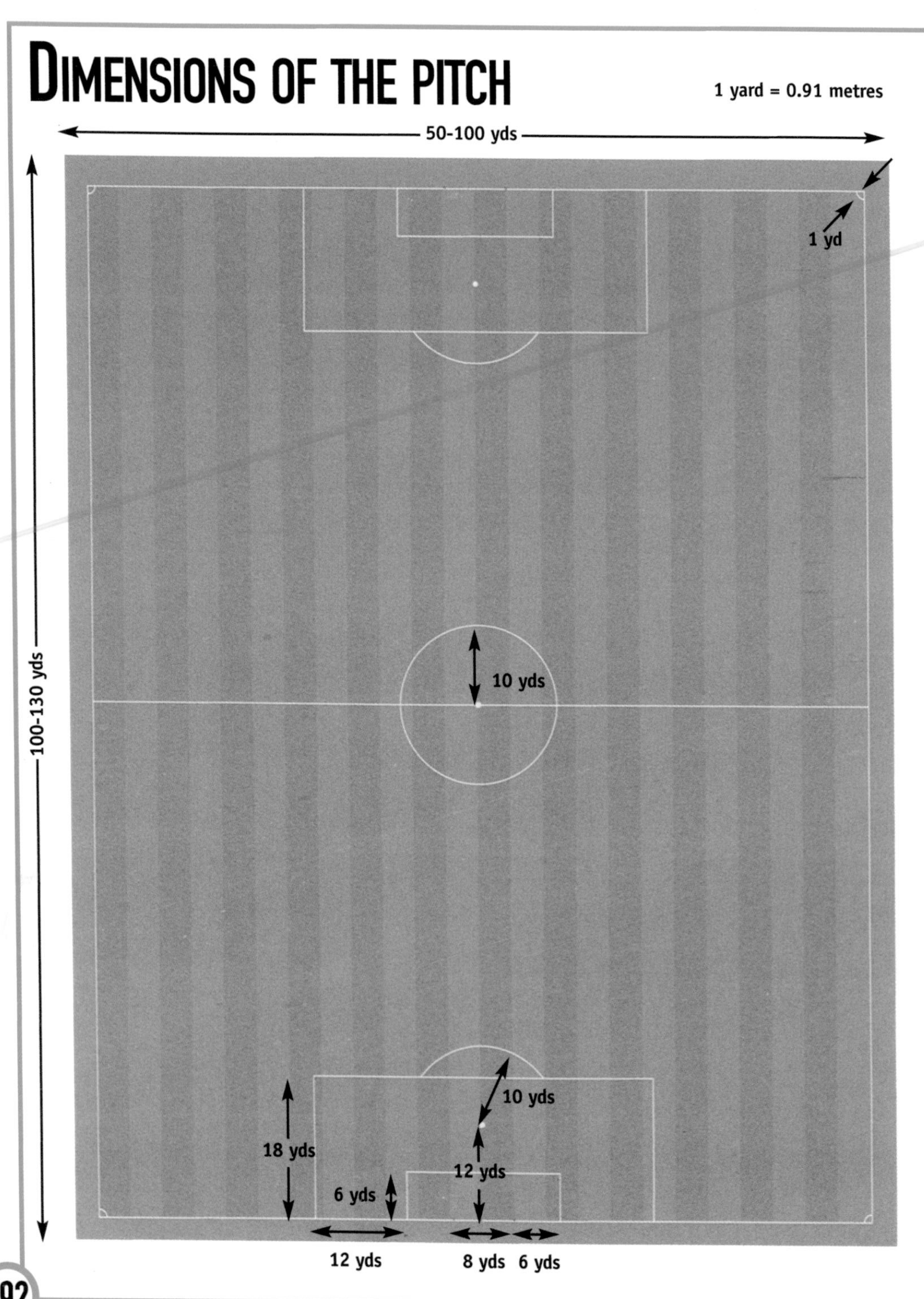